Activities and Study Gui

Marketing, 4e

James L. Burrow

Aubrey R. Fowler

SOUTH-WESTERN
CENGAGE Learning

Australia • Brazil • Japan • Korea • Mexico • Singapore • Spain • United Kingdom • United States

SOUTH-WESTERN
CENGAGE Learning

For product information and technology assistance, contact us at **Cengage Learning Academic Resource Center, 1-800-423-0563**.

For permission to use material from this text or product, submit all requests online at **www.cengage.com/permissions**. Further permissions questions can be emailed to **permissionrequest@cengage.com**.

ISBN-13: 978-1-285-06284-6

South-Western Cengage Learning
20 Channel Center Street
Boston, MA 02210
USA

Cengage Learning is a leading provider of customized learning solutions with office locations around the globe, including Singapore, the United Kingdom, Australia, Mexico, Brazil, and Japan. Locate your local office at: **www.cengage.com/global**.

Cengage Learning products are represented in Canada by Nelson Education, Ltd.

For your course and learning solutions, visit **ngl.cengage.com.**

Visit our company website at **www.cengage.com.**

Printed in the United States of America
Print Number: 01 Print Year: 2015

Contents

CHAPTER 1	***MARKETING TODAY AND TOMORROW***	***1***
Lesson 1.1	What Is Marketing?	1
Lesson 1.2	Business Needs Marketing	3
Lesson 1.3	The Marketing Concept	5
Lesson 1.4	The Changing Role of Marketing	7
CHAPTER 2	***SOCIALLY RESPONSIBLE MARKETING***	***9***
Lesson 2.1	The Impact of Marketing	9
Lesson 2.2	Criticisms of Marketing	11
Lesson 2.3	Increase Social Responsibility	13
CHAPTER 3	***MARKETING BEGINS WITH ECONOMICS***	***15***
Lesson 3.1	Scarcity and Private Enterprise	15
Lesson 3.2	The Law of Supply and Demand	17
Lesson 3.3	Types of Economic Competition	19
Lesson 3.4	Economic Utility	21
CHAPTER 4	***THE BASICS OF MARKETING***	***23***
Lesson 4.1	Changes in Today's Marketing	23
Lesson 4.2	Plan a Marketing Strategy	25
Lesson 4.3	Consumers and Competitors	27
Lesson 4.4	The Varied Role of Marketing	29

CHAPTER 5	***MARKETING INFORMATION AND RESEARCH***	***31***
Lesson 5.1	Understand the Need for Marketing Information	31
Lesson 5.2	Find and Manage Marketing Information	33
Lesson 5.3	Use Marketing Research	35
Lesson 5.4	Collect Primary Data	37
CHAPTER 6	***MARKETING STARTS WITH CUSTOMERS***	***39***
Lesson 6.1	Understand Consumer Behavior	39
Lesson 6.2	What Motivates Buyers?	41
Lesson 6.3	Influence Consumer Decisions	43
CHAPTER 7	***COMPETITION IS EVERYWHERE***	***45***
Lesson 7.1	Focus on Market Segments	45
Lesson 7.2	Position for Competitive Advantage	47
Lesson 7.3	Compete for Market Segments	49
Lesson 7.4	Learn about the Competition	51
CHAPTER 8	***SOCIAL MEDIA AND E-COMMERCE***	***53***
Lesson 8.1	Technolody, the Internet, and E-Commerce	53
Lesson 8.2	The Emergence of Social Media	55
Lesson 8.3	Social Media as a Marketing Tool	57
CHAPTER 9	***DEVELOP A MARKETING STRATEGY AND MARKETING PLAN***	***59***
Lesson 9.1	Elements of a Marketing Strategy	59
Lesson 9.2	Marketing Mix Alternatives	61
Lesson 9.3	Consumer Purchase Classifications	63
Lesson 9.4	Marketing Planning	65
Lesson 9.5	Develop a Marketing Plan	67

CHAPTER 10	***DEVELOP SUCCESSFUL PRODUCTS***	*69*
Lesson 10.1	Start with a Product	69
Lesson 10.2	Components of the Product Mix	71
Lesson 10.3	Products for Consumers and Businesses	73
Lesson 10.4	New Product Development	75
CHAPTER 11	***SERVICES NEED MARKETING***	*77*
Lesson 11.1	What Are Services?	77
Lesson 11.2	Classify Services and Evaluate Quality	79
Lesson 11.3	Develop a Service Marketing Mix	81
CHAPTER 12	***BUSINESS-TO-BUSINESS MARKETING***	*83*
Lesson 12.1	Business-to-Business Exchanges	83
Lesson 12.2	Make Business Purchase Decisions	85
Lesson 12.3	Business Purchasing Procedures	87
Lesson 12.4	Retail Purchasing	89
CHAPTER 13	***DISTRIBUTION***	*91*
Lesson 13.1	Marketing Through Distribution	91
Lesson 13.2	Distribution Channels	93
Lesson 13.3	The Role of Wholesaling	95
Lesson 13.4	The Role of Retailing	97
Lesson 13.5	Physical Distribution	99
CHAPTER 14	***DETERMINE THE BEST PRICE***	*101*
Lesson 14.1	The Economics of Price Decisions	101
Lesson 14.2	Develop Pricing Procedures	103
Lesson 14.3	Pricing Based on Market Conditions	105

CHAPTER 15	***PROMOTION***	***107***
Lesson 15.1	Promotion as a Form of Communication	107
Lesson 15.2	Types of Promotion	109
Lesson 15.3	The Promotional Plan	111
CHAPTER 16	***ADVERTISING***	***113***
Lesson 16.1	What Is Advertising?	113
Lesson 16.2	Plan Advertising	115
Lesson 16.3	Create and Evaluate Advertising	117
CHAPTER 17	***SELLING***	***119***
Lesson 17.1	The Value of Selling	119
Lesson 17.2	Prepare for Effective Selling	121
Lesson 17.3	The Selling Process and Sales Support	123
CHAPTER 18	***MARKETING IN A GLOBAL ECONOMY***	***125***
Lesson 18.1	The Expanding World Economy	125
Lesson 18.2	How Businesses Get Involved	127
Lesson 18.3	Understand International Markets	129
CHAPTER 19	***MANAGE RISKS***	***131***
Lesson 19.1	Assess Business Risks	131
Lesson 19.2	Identify Marketing Risks	133
Lesson 19.3	Manage Marketing Risks	135
CHAPTER 20	***FINANCE MARKETING ACTIVITIES***	***137***
Lesson 20.1	Marketing Affects Business Finances	137
Lesson 20.2	Tools for Financial Planning	139
Lesson 20.3	Budget for Marketing Activities	141

CHAPTER 21	***ENTREPRENEURSHIP AND MARKETING***	***143***
Lesson 21.1	**Understand Entrepreneurship**	**143**
Lesson 21.2	**Characteristics of Entrepreneurs**	**145**
Lesson 21.3	**Business Ownership Opportunities**	**147**
Lesson 21.4	**Legal Needs of Entrepreneurs**	**149**
Lesson 21.5	**Develop a Business Plan**	**151**
CHAPTER 22	***TAKE CONTROL WITH MANAGEMENT***	***153***
Lesson 22.1	**The Functions of Management**	**153**
Lesson 22.2	**Manage with a Marketing Plan**	**155**
Lesson 22.3	**The Marketing Manager Role**	**157**
CHAPTER 23	***PLAN YOUR FUTURE IN MARKETING***	***159***
Lesson 23.1	**Benefits of a Marketing Career**	**159**
Lesson 23.2	**Employment Levels in Marketing**	**161**
Lesson 23.3	**Marketing Education and Career Paths**	**163**
Lesson 23.4	**Begin Career Planning**	**165**

Name ______________________________ Date __________ Class ____________________

Lesson 1.1 What Is Marketing?

LESSON QUIZ

Directions For each of the following statements, if the statement is true, write a T on the answer line; if the statement is false, write an F on the answer line.

_____ 1. Millions of companies today have marketing as their primary business activity.

_____ 2. Marketing activities today are completed in much the same way they have always been done.

_____ 3. Developing marketing skills can actually help you be a more effective consumer.

_____ 4. Credit card companies are directly involved in marketing.

_____ 5. Marketing activities can be categorized within four functions.

_____ 6. Marketing activities are completed by profit-making businesses but not by nonprofit businesses.

_____ 7. A business is involved in marketing when it communicates the value of products to prospective customers.

Directions For each of the following items, decide which choice best completes the statement. Write the letter that identifies your choice on the answer line.

_____ 8. Successful businesses develop an approach to marketing planning that responds to
A. new products
B. trends in the industry
C. the needs of customers
D. every situation

_____ 9. By studying marketing, you will learn
A. how businesses use marketing to increase their effectiveness and profits
B. how new businesses are established
C. how products are manufactured
D. why consumers are usually misled by marketing

_____10. Distribution includes
A. creating a budget for marketing activities
B. completing research to develop new products
C. advertising and other forms of promotion
D. moving products from the producer to locations where customers can buy them

_____11. Marketing-information management includes
A. obtaining market information to improve decision making
B. establishing the best price for a product or service
C. developing an effective sales presentation
D. improving the efficiency of product delivery

Activity 1 • Apply the Marketing Functions

Directions Describe how the following business and organizations would use each of the nine marketing functions.

	Bank	Professional Sports Team	Jewelry Store	Public Library
Market Planning				
Product and Service Management				
Distribution				
Pricing				
Promotion				
Selling				
Marketing-Information Management				
Financing				
Risk Management				

Name ______________________________ Date __________ Class ____________________

Lesson 1.2 Business Needs Marketing

LESSON QUIZ

Directions For each of the following statements, if the statement is true, write a T on the answer line; if the statement is false, write an F on the answer line.

_____ 1. All business functions contribute in specific ways to the success of the business.

_____ 2. Marketing is particularly important when businesses produce a low-quality product.

_____ 3. Specialization of labor results in the production of large quantities of a product.

_____ 4. Self-sufficient people bartered for goods they needed.

_____ 5. Marketing has existed since businesses began exchanging goods.

_____ 6. A money system was developed to assist with the exchange process.

_____ 7. A new or small business does not need to coordinate its business functions.

Directions For each of the following items, decide which choice best completes the statement. Write the letter that identifies your choice on the answer line.

_____ 8. Self-sufficient people
- A. do not rely on others for the things they need to survive
- B. find or produce the food and materials they and their families need
- C. face challenges due to poor weather, competition with others, sickness, or lack of skills
- D. all of the above

_____ 9. In order to barter, both parties
- A. must want what the other party has
- B. must have money
- C. must travel
- D. must have most needs satisfied already

_____10. Central markets were usually located
- A. where both producers and consumers lived
- B. where people frequently traveled
- C. where facilities to store products already existed
- D. all of the above

_____11. Operations includes
- A. obtaining, transporting and storing products
- B. maintaining buildings and equipment
- C. preparing and maintaining records
- D. all of the above

Activity 1 • Bartering

Directions In the small town of Woodville, people still barter to obtain the products they need. Use the information below to make trades that will satisfy the town's residents. Identify the trades that each individual must make to acquire the item he or she wants. Enter the name of each person they must trade with in the boxes on the same level in the order in which the trades must occur.

	Makes	**Wants**
Sara	Bread	Vegetables
Max	Meat	Bread
Lynne	Fabric	Bread
Jason	Fruit	Fabric
Melanie	Bread	Meat
Thomas	Vegetables	Fruit

Sara			
Max			
Lynne			
Jason			
Melanie			
Thomas			

Name ______________________________ Date __________ Class ______________

Lesson 1.3 The Marketing Concept

LESSON QUIZ

Directions For each of the following statements, if the statement is true, write a T on the answer line; if the statement is false, write an F on the answer line.

_____ 1. Marketing has always been an important part of business.

_____ 2. The most successful businesses consider customers' needs as they produce and market their products and services.

_____ 3. In the early 1900s the biggest challenges most businesses faced was getting the products from the places where they were produced to where customers purchased them.

_____ 4. The marketing concept works for nonprofit organizations such as colleges and hospitals as well as for businesses whose goal is to make a profit.

_____ 5. A marketing mix is the blending of three marketing elements—product, distribution, and promotion.

_____ 6. Companies that follow the marketing concept cannot be concerned about the amount of profit they make.

_____ 7. Price is the actual cost that a business incurs to produce and market the product.

Directions For each of the following items, decide which choice best completes the statement. Write the letter that identifies your choice on the answer line.

_____ 8. As consumers increased their standard of living and had more money to spend, the demand for newer and better products
A. increased
B. decreased
C. remained the same
D. varied widely

_____ 9. Which of these activities must a business accomplish in order to use the marketing concept successfully?
A. identify customer needs
B. develop and market products or services
C. operate the business profitably
D. all of the above

_____10. Businesses that do not use the marketing concept
A. are not concerned about understanding customer needs
B. sell more products
C. are better able to control costs
D. earn higher profits

Activity 1 • Recycling Sells

Directions As the marketing manager of a large manufacturing facility, you developed a marketing research program to determine consumers' responsiveness to using products identified as "manufactured with recycled materials." The results have indicated an 83 percent approval rating from consumers who purchase products that carry a recycling symbol on the package. Based on that result, you believe the company should consider using recycled materials.

Write a memo to the chief operating officer of the company explaining the study and its results. Encourage management to consider your recommendation and to use it as an important part of the marketing strategy. Be sure to indicate how this tactic can be used as a part of each marketing mix element—product, price, promotion, and distribution.

____

____

____

____

____

____

____

____

____

Activity 2 • Who's in the Market?

Directions Develop specific descriptions of two different potential markets for each of the following businesses.

1. A health and fitness club: ____

____

____

2. A cruise ship: ____

____

____

3. A fast-copy printing business: ____

____

____

4. A tax accountant: ____

____

____

Name ______________________ Date ________ Class ______________

Lesson 1.4 The Changing Role of Marketing

LESSON QUIZ

Directions For each of the following statements, if the statement is true, write a T on the answer line; if the statement is false, write an F on the answer line.

_____ 1. During the Production Era, production processes were very complex and many product choices were available.

_____ 2. During the Sales Era, transportation systems were not well developed.

_____ 3. During the Marketing Department Era companies increasingly relied on a variety of marketing activities to find ways to expand markets and sell more products.

_____ 4. Empowered customer service employees have the authority to solve many customer problems.

_____ 5. After changing a great deal in the first half of the 20th century, the role of marketing in businesses has remained the same since that time.

_____ 6. Marketing includes distribution, pricing, credit, and customer service.

_____ 7. Marketing can help the business be more profitable by coordinating activities and controlling costs.

Directions For each of the following items, decide which choice best completes the statement. Write the letter that identifies your choice on the answer line.

_____ 8. Select the option that correctly identifies the development sequence of the philosophy of marketing.
- A. Production Era, Sales Era, Marketing Department Era, and Marketing Concept Era
- B. Marketing Department Era, Production Era, Sales Era, and Marketing Concept Era
- C. Production Era, Marketing Department Era, Sales Era, and Marketing Concept Era
- D. Sales Era, Production Era, Marketing Concept Era, and Marketing Department Era

_____ 9. During the Marketing Concept Era,
- A. marketing became the work of more than one department
- B. advertising was used as a means to convince customers to buy products they may not need
- C. many new marketing activities were developed
- D. customer needs were more important than profit

_____10. Relationship marketing focuses on
- A. developing effective working relationships in employee teams
- B. giving employees the authority to solve many customer problems
- C. identifying new customers to replace older, less satisfied customers
- D. developing loyal customers who continue to purchase from the business for a long period of time

Activity 1 • Competition in the Air

Directions The airline industry in the United States has, in recent years, struggled to make a profit. Describe some of the ways various airlines have altered the elements of the marketing mix to try to remain competitive. Explain whether or not you think the changes reflect a commitment to the marketing concept.

Activity 2 • Meet Customer Needs

Directions Select an item you own and use regularly. Identify 10 ways the product specifically meets your needs as a consumer.

Name ______________________________ Date __________ Class ____________________

Lesson 2.1 The Impact of Marketing

LESSON QUIZ

Directions For each of the following statements, if the statement is true, write a T on the answer line; if the statement is false, write an F on the answer line.

_____ 1. Businesses that use the marketing concept benefit more from marketing than companies that do not.

_____ 2. Marketing helps a business satisfy customer wants and needs.

_____ 3. While businesses see direct benefits from the use of marketing, individual consumers do not.

_____ 4. Marketing skills can be valuable to people who are not directly employed in the field of marketing.

_____ 5. Marketing identifies consumer needs that are not satisfied.

_____ 6. When the marketing concept is used, the cost of production and product prices increase.

_____ 7. Marketing activities are essential for international trade.

Directions For each of the following items, decide which choice best completes the statement. Write the letter that identifies your choice on the answer line.

_____ 8. Keeping customers satisfied
- A. is not important because customers will usually keep shopping until they find the lowest prices
- B. is important because they are more likely to continue to purchase from the business
- C. is not as cost-effective to a business as attracting new customers
- D. none of the above is correct

_____ 9. As a result of marketing, you can
- A. choose from a wide variety of products and services
- B. buy from businesses that respond to your needs
- C. develop personal style and relationships
- D. all of the above

_____10. Marketing skills help individuals to
- A. make dinner
- B. exercise
- C. find employment
- D. follow instructions

_____11. To encourage international trade, marketing
- A. identifies new markets for a company's products
- B. identifies more efficient production methods
- C. employs workers at lower wage rates
- D. all of the above

Activity 1 • Opportunities in the Marketing Field

Directions Look in the employment section of your local newspaper or its affiliated website. Identify three positions that require marketing skills. Describe the marketing skills that are required and the responsibilities of the positions.

Activity 2 • Naming Rights

Directions Identify the businesses that named the sports facilities in or near your city. Use the library or Internet to identify the amount of money paid by the businesses. How do you believe the businesses benefit from that investment?

Name ______________________________ Date __________ Class ______________

Lesson 2.2 Criticisms of Marketing

LESSON QUIZ

Directions For each of the following statements, if the statement is true, write a T on the answer line; if the statement is false, write an F on the answer line.

_____ 1. The use of marketing always has positive results.

_____ 2. Marketing activities, including the use of promotion, cannot actually increase the sales of products and services.

_____ 3. The average cost of all marketing activities is about 50 percent of the price of products.

_____ 4. Marketing can be used to misrepresent poor products.

_____ 5. Marketing has been used effectively to help solve serious social issues.

_____ 6. Green marketing consists of marketing activities designed to satisfy customer needs without negatively impacting the environment.

_____ 7. A positive contribution of marketing is to be able to transport products in short supply to locations where they are needed.

Directions For each of the following items, decide which choice best completes the statement. Write the letter that identifies your choice on the answer line.

_____ 8. Which of these is not a common complaint about marketing?
A. causes unneeded purchases
B. causes social problems
C. increases public awareness
D. wastes money

_____ 9. The long-term results of poor marketing can include
A. reduced costs
B. dissatisfied customers
C. less competition
D. higher profits

_____10. Effective marketing results in
A. higher prices in the long run
B. higher costs and lower profits
C. lower sales volume and greater competition
D. lower prices of products and services for consumers

_____11. Social problems
A. should be addressed by marketing
B. are usually made worse by marketers
C. affect only a small part of the population so are not a concern of marketers
D. all of the above

Activity 1 • Social Issues

Directions Identify a social issue that can be affected by marketing. Design a poster that could be used in a promotional campaign directed at calling attention to the issue.

Activity 2 • Finding Data

Directions The U.S. Census Bureau maintains demographic data, which it posts on its Internet site at www.census.gov. Use the Internet or library to find answers to the following questions.

What is the population of your city?	
What is the population of your county?	
What is the average age of the population in your state?	
What percentage of the population in your state is male?	
What is the size of the average family in your state?	
What is the size of the average household in your state?	
What percentage of the population in your state graduated from high school?	
What percentage of the population in your state graduated from college?	
How many veterans live in your state?	
What is the second most common language spoken in your state?	
What is the largest industry in your county?	
What is the mean household income in your state?	

Name ______________________________ Date __________ Class ____________________

Lesson 2.3 Increase Social Responsibility

LESSON QUIZ

Directions For each of the following statements, if the statement is true, write a T on the answer line; if the statement is false, write an F on the answer line.

_____ 1. Today there is a greater expectation for businesses to be socially responsible and to aid in solving the problems facing society.

_____ 2. Social problems often lead to increased government regulation of business or increases in taxes to pay for programs designed to solve the problems.

_____ 3. The Better Business Bureau is a business protection organization sponsored by consumer organizations.

_____ 4. Consumer organizations encourage others to purchase products from boycotted companies.

_____ 5. Organizations and industries often develop a code of ethics to punish dishonest and improper conduct.

_____ 6. It is not always easy to agree whether an activity is ethical or unethical, but people expect ethical business behavior.

_____ 7. Improper marketing can cause harm to customers.

Directions For each of the following items, decide which choice best completes the statement. Write the letter that identifies your choice on the answer line.

_____ 8. Organized actions of groups of consumers seeking to increase their influence on business practices is

A. consumerism
B. social responsibility
C. a consumer group
D. a social issue

_____ 9. Taking personal responsibility for actions is known as

A. integrity
B. self-regulation
C. honesty
D. self-control

_____10. Unethical behavior of marketers

A. always harms consumers
B. is always illegal
C. is never illegal
D. may also be illegal

Activity 1 • Loss Leaders

Directions Many grocery stores and supermarkets use "loss leaders" to get consumers into their stores. Loss leaders are popular, regularly purchased items that are sold well below their usual price (examples could include milk, soft drinks, and bread). Businesspeople using loss leaders believe that when people come to the store to buy the inexpensive item, they will buy many more items at regular or even higher prices. Consider the practice of using loss leaders. Then prepare two position statements using the following headings.

1. I believe the use of loss leaders is an appropriate business practice because. . .

____

____

____

2. I believe the use of loss leaders is a deceptive business practice because. . .

____

____

____

Activity 2 • Regulation of E-Commerce

Directions With the growth of e-commerce, there is a growing concern that some e-commerce businesses are not socially responsible and that consumers can be harmed by their unethical or inappropriate practices. Use the Internet to identify one example of each of the following types of regulation for e-commerce. Write a short description of the type of business practice that is the focus of the regulation.

1. Government regulation

____

____

____

2. Self-regulation

____

____

____

3. Consumer actions

____

____

____

Name ______________________________ Date __________ Class______________________

Lesson 3.1 Scarcity and Private Enterprise

LESSON QUIZ

Directions For each of the following statements, if the statement is true, write a T on the answer line; if the statement is false, write an F on the answer line.

_____ 1. The marketing process is more scientific than creative.

_____ 2. There are enough resources available in the world to meet everyone's wants and needs.

_____ 3. In a free enterprise economy, resources are free so anyone can obtain them.

_____ 4. The U.S. economy has many characteristics of a private enterprise economy.

_____ 5. Consumers create demand for products when they select the ones they think will provide the greatest satisfaction for the price.

_____ 6. The quantity of a product that producers are willing and able to provide at a specific price is known as demand.

_____ 7. In a private enterprise economy, the government uses laws and regulations to protect society from harmful decisions made by producers and consumers.

Directions For each of the following items, decide which choice best completes the statement. Write the letter that identifies your choice on the answer line.

_____ 8. The basic economic problem is
A. scarcity
B. monopolies
C. consumers
D. capitalism

_____ 9. Which needs are satisfied and how resources are distributed in a country depend on
A. raw materials
B. consumer education
C. product prices
D. the country's economic system

_____10. A decision to use resources in a way that results in the greatest profit for the producer is known as
A. free enterprise
B. scarcity
C. the profit motive
D. value

_____11. In a private enterprise economy, the success or failure of a business is determined primarily by
A. consumer demand
B. state and federal laws and regulations
C. the decisions each business makes
D. competitors' actions

Activity 1 • Find the Resources

Directions In the first column, identify a location (country or region) where a manufacturing business can obtain the following raw or manufactured materials. In the second column, identify a product that you or your family might purchase that includes the resource in its production.

	Source	Used In
Wood	____________	____________
	____________	____________
Aluminum	____________	____________
	____________	____________
Steel	____________	____________
	____________	____________
Granite	____________	____________
	____________	____________
Corn	____________	____________
	____________	____________
Sugar	____________	____________
	____________	____________
Water	____________	____________
	____________	____________
Glass	____________	____________
	____________	____________
Silk	____________	____________
	____________	____________
Coal	____________	____________
	____________	____________
Oil	____________	____________
	____________	____________

Name ______________________________ Date __________ Class ______________

Lesson 3.2 The Law of Supply and Demand

LESSON QUIZ

Directions For each of the following statements, if the statement is true, write a T on the answer line; if the statement is false, write an F on the answer line.

_____ 1. Understanding economics helps consumers and producers use their resources effectively.

_____ 2. Macroeconomics studies how individuals make decisions about what to produce and what to consume.

_____ 3. Consumers will pay more for a product if the supply of that product increases.

_____ 4. A supply curve demonstrates the relationship between price and the quantity of a product supplied.

_____ 5. As competition increases, businesses find greater opportunities for success.

_____ 6. As the price of a product increases, businesses will produce more of that product if possible.

_____ 7. A supply curve and a demand curve should never intersect.

Directions For each of the following items, decide which choice best completes the statement. Write the letter that identifies your choice on the answer line.

_____ 8. The point at which supply and demand are equal for a product is known as
A. the demand curve
B. the supply curve
C. the market price
D. Supply and demand are never equal

_____ 9. Marketers are most interested in
A. microeconomics
B. macroeconomics
C. price increases
D. government regulation

_____10. If there are no alternative products to satisfy consumers' needs,
A. the supply will be large
B. the price will be low
C. supply and demand are unaffected
D. consumers will pay more

_____11. All of the consumers who will purchase a particular product or service comprise a(n)
A. supply
B. economic market
C. economy
D. market group

Activity 1 • Supply and Demand

Directions Using the information from the following chart, construct a supply curve and a demand curve on the graph. Circle the point on the graph that identifies the market price. Estimate the market price and quantity.

PRICE	QUANTITY DEMANDED	QUANTITY SUPPLIED
$ 5.00	10,000	2,000
10.00	8,500	3,000
15.00	6,000	5,000
20.00	3,000	7,500
25.00	1,000	9,000

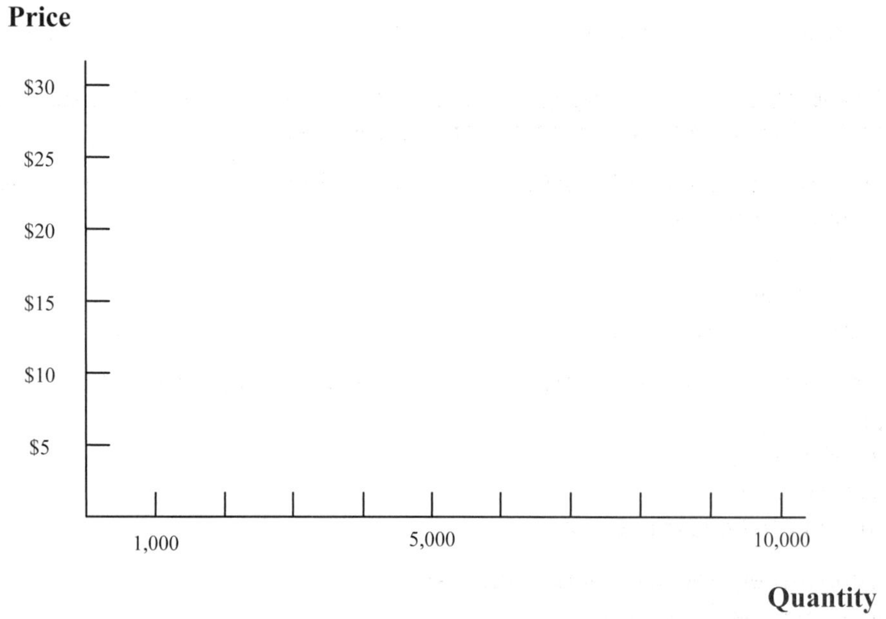

Estimate of market price $ ____________

Estimate of market quantity ____________

Name ______________________________ Date __________ Class ______________________

Lesson 3.3 Types of Economic Competition

LESSON QUIZ

Directions For each of the following statements, if the statement is true, write a T on the answer line; if the statement is false, write an F on the answer line.

_____ 1. In pure competition, a large number of suppliers offer very similar products.

_____ 2. A business in monopolistic competition has no control over price if it wants to sell its products.

_____ 3. In a monopoly, customers will pay a higher price because there are no alternative products to those of the supplier.

_____ 4. A cable television company usually operates in a pure competition environment.

_____ 5. The airline industry is an example of an oligopoly.

_____ 6. The most common type of economic competition facing most businesses is pure competition.

_____ 7. Businesses in monopolistic competition should focus on making their products different from and better than competitors' products .

_____ 8. Each product in a specific market has its own supply and demand curves.

Directions For each of the following items, decide which choice best completes the statement. Write the letter that identifies your choice on the answer line.

_____ 9. The market environment in which a business without competitors operates is
A. pure competition
B. an oligopoly
C. a monopoly
D. monopolistic competition

_____10. The market environment in which most retail businesses operate is
A. pure competition
B. an oligopoly
C. a monopoly
D. monopolistic competition

_____11. As a consumer, you will usually choose the
A. least expensive option
B. option providing the most satisfaction at the best value
C. option that provides the highest quality
D. most readily available option

_____12. In a market where demand exceeds supply
A. consumers can expect to pay higher prices
B. businesses will want to increase supply
C. some consumers will not be able to satisfy their needs
D. all are correct

Activity 1 • Economic Competition

Directions Companies will market products or services in quite different ways depending on the type of economic competition they face. A business in a monopoly will have a different marketing mix from one in pure competition. Select one of the following businesses and use it for the entire activity: car rental business, airline, restaurant, construction company, gas station, supermarket, bank, or recording studio. Using the chart, describe how each part of the marketing mix would be different for the business in each type of economic competition.

Business: ______________________________

	Type of Economic Competition			
Marketing Mix Element	**Monopoly**	**Pure Competition**	**Oligopoly**	**Monopolistic Competition**
Product				
Price				
Distribution				
Promotion				

Name ____ Date ____________ Class________________________

Lesson 3.4 Economic Utility

LESSON QUIZ

Directions For each of the following statements, if the statement is true, write a T on the answer line; if the statement is false, write an F on the answer line.

_____ 1. Form utility results from changes in the tangible parts of a product or service.

_____ 2. A business that schedules its hours to better meet consumer needs provides place utility.

_____ 3. Offering auto leases rather than requiring customers to pay the full purchase price provides possession utility.

_____ 4. Convenience stores open 24 hours a day usually provide both time and place utility.

_____ 5. Possession utility does not occur until the consumer owns the product.

_____ 6. A business that mails movie rentals to consumers rather than requiring them to visit its store is primarily improving form.

_____ 7. Improving products through analyzing economic utility supports the marketing concept.

Directions For each of the following items, decide which choice best completes the statement. Write the letter that identifies your choice on the answer line.

_____ 8. The amount of satisfaction a consumer receives from the consumption of a particular product or service is
A. form utility
B. possession utility
C. time utility
D. economic utility

_____ 9. Packaging milk into smaller containers to meet the demand of people who live alone is an example of
A. form utility
B. possession utility
C. time utility
D. place utility

_____10. Offering coupons or sale prices for a product provides
A. form utility
B. possession utility
C. time utility
D. place utility

_____11. When economic utility is improved
A. prices charged by businesses will increase
B. consumers will have fewer choices
C. customer satisfaction improves as well
D. competition will be greater

Activity 1 • Communicate About Economic Utility

Directions Economic utility is an important concept for marketers because it is used to add value to a product or service to improve customer satisfaction. Businesses communicate the ways in which they are providing economic utility through promotions and other forms of information. Each of the forms of economic utility is identified in the table below. Review information about products and services using magazines, the Internet, and other company information. For each type, select one example of information that describes a product or service feature related to that type of economic utility. Attach a copy of the information (or prepare a summary if a copy is not available). In the space provided develop a brief statement describing how customer satisfaction is improved as a result.

EXAMPLE OF FORM UTILITY **Reasons for improved customer satisfaction:** ________________ ________________ ________________ ________________ ________________ ________________ ________________ ________________	**EXAMPLE OF TIME UTILITY** **Reasons for improved customer satisfaction:** ________________ ________________ ________________ ________________ ________________ ________________ ________________ ________________
EXAMPLE OF PLACE UTILITY **Reasons for improved customer satisfaction:** ________________ ________________ ________________ ________________ ________________ ________________ ________________ ________________	**EXAMPLE OF POSSESSION UTILITY** **Reasons for improved customer satisfaction:** ________________ ________________ ________________ ________________ ________________ ________________ ________________ ________________

Name ______________________________ Date __________ Class ______________

Lesson 4.1 Changes in Today's Marketing

LESSON QUIZ

Directions For each of the following statements, if the statement is true, write a T on the answer line; if the statement is false, write an F on the answer line.

_____ 1. Marketing has changed very little from the way businesses used it in the past.

_____ 2. The earliest use of marketing was to move products from producer to consumer.

_____ 3. Marketing is more effective when it is integrated into other business activities.

_____ 4. Most marketing strategies are developed as a result of problems businesses encounter.

_____ 5. Market opportunities include new markets and ways to improve a company's offerings in current markets.

_____ 6. In the past, many businesses reduced marketing efforts when faced with financial problems.

_____ 7. Spending money on marketing reduces a company's profit in the long run.

_____ 8. The marketing concept keeps the main focus on customers' needs during the planning, production, distribution, and promotion of a product or service.

Directions For each of the following items, decide which choice best completes the statement. Write the letter that identifies your choice on the answer line.

_____ 9. When a company integrates its marketing efforts, it
- A. involves marketing in all important business decisions
- B. uses marketing as a problem-solving tool only
- C. makes marketing an independent part of the business
- D. views marketing as an expense rather than an investment

_____10. Businesses that adopt the marketing concept
- A. reduce the number of marketing activities they complete
- B. separate marketing planning from other business plans
- C. use a totally new approach to thinking and planning
- D. will be successful if they produce a quality product

_____11. A business takes a big risk when it is unwilling to
- A. cut costs
- B. study the needs of its customers
- C. increase promotion
- D. all of the above

_____12. Today's marketers are continuously looking for
- A. market opportunities
- B. ways to harm competitors
- C. less expensive production methods
- D. chances to increase product prices

Activity 1 • Home on the Range

Directions In America's past, horses, like marketing, served a different purpose. In the Wild West, horses were a means of transportation and a necessary part of a ranch's livestock. Compare how horses were marketed in the past with the way a dude ranch would be marketed today.

PAST	PRESENT
Few Activities	Variety of Activities
Independent	Integrated
Problem-solver	Opportunity-Provider
Expense	Investment

Name ______________________________ Date __________ Class ______________

Lesson 4.2 Plan a Marketing Strategy

LESSON QUIZ

Directions For each of the following statements, if the statement is true, write a T on the answer line; if the statement is false, write an F on the answer line.

_____ 1. Without the marketing concept, a business will develop a product or service and then decide how to market it.

_____ 2. Various groups of customers may have different needs.

_____ 3. Product planning must be done before any marketing decisions are made.

_____ 4. The marketing mix combines product, distribution, price, and promotion.

_____ 5. A market segment is a group of similar consumers within a larger market.

_____ 6. A business that follows the marketing concept focuses its business planning on increasing sales.

Directions For each of the following items, decide which choice best completes the statement. Write the letter that identifies your choice on the answer line.

_____ 7. If a company understands the marketing concept, its first step will be to
A. identify potential customers and their needs
B. develop a product
C. develop a marketing mix
D. distribute the product

_____ 8. Businesses that do not follow the marketing concept believe
A. consumers do not know what they want
B. they can influence consumer needs with well-designed products
C. most consumers are similar in terms of their needs
D. all are correct

_____ 9. A clearly defined segment of the market to which a business wants to appeal is called a
A. target market
B. market segment
C. marketing mix
D. marketing opportunity

_____10. Which of the following is not a part of the product mix element?
A. the actual physical product
B. related services
C. product uses
D. transportation

_____11. Probably the most difficult marketing decision to understand and plan is
A. product
B. distribution
C. price
D. promotion

Activity 1 • Slogan Mix and Match

Directions The goal of promotion is to direct a meaningful message to a target market about an attribute of the product or service. That is frequently done by the creation of a slogan designed to make a memorable impression on consumers. Some slogans become so well known that they live on after the product no longer exists or the business develops a new slogan. For each slogan in the table below, select the company from the last column you believe used that slogan to promote its products. Place the letter identifying the company in front of the correct slogan. Based on your knowledge of the product and the slogan, identify the market segment that was being targeted with a short description in the Target Market column.

Answers		Slogan	Target Market		Companies
________	1.	Think outside the bun	____________	a.	Coca-Cola
________	2.	Don't leave home without it	____________	b.	Microsoft
________	3.	Just do it	____________	c.	Volkswagen
________	4.	Be all you can be	____________	d.	Nike
________	5.	Mmm mmm good	____________	e.	Taco Bell
________	6.	Open happiness	____________	f.	United Airlines
________	7.	Drivers wanted	____________	g.	American Express
________	8.	You're in good hands	____________	h.	U.S. Army
________	9.	Fly the friendly skies	____________	i.	Campbell's
________	10.	Your potential. Our passion.	____________	j.	Allstate

Activity 2 • Where You Belong

Directions Describe the market segment that you identify with the most when you make frequent purchases. Identify common characteristics and similarities of people in the market.

____

____

____

____

____

Name ______________________________ Date __________ Class ______________________

Lesson 4.3 Consumers and Competitors

LESSON QUIZ

Directions For each of the following statements, if the statement is true, write a T on the answer line; if the statement is false, write an F on the answer line.

_____ 1. Consumers want to choose the alternative that requires the least amount of money.

_____ 2. A consumer may be aware of a product but will not purchase it until a need exists.

_____ 3. Consumers always spend a great deal of time and want a large amount of information when evaluating alternative choices.

_____ 4. Most decisions to purchase are made before the consumer evaluates choices.

_____ 5. The most difficult type of competition businesses face is a market in which they compete with others offering very similar products.

_____ 6. Customers using the products and services of a monopoly business often become dissatisfied with their lack of choice.

_____ 7. Companies that use the marketing concept do not focus on specific groups of customers, but rather on all consumers in general.

Directions For each of the following items, decide which choice best completes the statement. Write the letter that identifies your choice on the answer line.

_____ 8. When consumers are restricted in their choice of products, reducing the need for companies to worry about price or promotion, this is known as

A. oligopoly
B. monopoly
C. pure competition
D. monopolistic competition

_____ 9. The consumer decision-making process begins when you

A. determine the satisfaction the decision creates
B. identify possible solutions
C. recognize a need
D. evaluate options

_____10. The most important type of research for most businesses is the study of

A. competitors' products and prices
B. ways to reduce costs
C. new products
D. potential and current customers

_____11. Companies in _______________ find the marketing concept to be of most value.

A. monopolistic competition
B. pure competition
C. a monopoly
D. an oligopoly

Activity 1 • Decisions, Decisions

Directions A vacation is meant to be fun, but it also means making plans. Planning a good vacation requires decisions. You can make decisions about your vacation before you leave home. Use the decision-making process to plan a vacation that doesn't cost more than $500.

Recognize a need.

Identify alternatives.

Evaluate choices.

Make a decision.

Determine satisfaction.

Name ______________________ Date ____________ Class ______________

Lesson 4.4 The Varied Role of Marketing

LESSON QUIZ

Directions For each of the following statements, if the statement is true, write a T on the answer line; if the statement is false, write an F on the answer line.

_____ 1. All businesses need to place the same amount of emphasis on each of the four marketing mix elements.

_____ 2. Because producers and manufacturers do not sell directly to final consumers, they do not need to understand and respond to consumer needs.

_____ 3. Producers and manufacturers need to be concerned about the needs of other businesses in the channel of distribution.

_____ 4. Customers will blame the manufacturer rather than other channel members if a product does not meet their needs.

_____ 5. Most service businesses do not use a channel of distribution.

_____ 6. Distribution planning is important to service businesses because the service must be available where and when the customer wants it.

_____ 7. A government agency is an example of a non-business organization.

_____ 8. Because nonprofit organizations do not have to be concerned about sales and expenses, they do not benefit a great deal from marketing.

Directions For each of the following items, decide which choice best completes the statement. Write the letter that identifies your choice on the answer line.

_____ 9. Which of the following businesses would not be a part of a channel of distribution?
A. producer
B. retailer
C. wholesaler
D. All would be a part of a distribution channel.

_____ 10. Retailers are responsible for most final _________ decisions.
A. product
B. pricing
C. distribution
D. promotion

_____ 11. The price of a service is difficult to compare because
A. a wholesale business is usually involved
B. different businesses may offer the service in a different way
C. the business has little control over the price
D. service businesses do not sell a wide variety of products

Activity 1 • Which Channel?

Directions Shelly designs and produces ceramic pottery. She wants to market her pottery but does not want to open her own retail store. She is considering three different distribution methods: (1) selling through local craft shops, (2) setting up a booth at weekend fairs and festivals to sell her products, (3) creating an Internet site to market her products and using a parcel service to ship the products she sells. Describe the channel of distribution and how marketing will be different for each alternative.

Method 1

____

____

____

Method 2

____

____

____

Method 3

____

____

____

Activity 2 • College Marketing

Directions Many high school students plan and prepare carefully to get accepted into the college of their choice. Colleges market themselves carefully to high school students and their parents to get the number of acceptable applications they need. They compete with many other colleges for top students. Select two colleges that actively recruit students from your high school. Gather information on the activities each college uses as a part of its marketing plan and the type of information they provide. Determine if they appear to be recruiting the same types of students. In the space below describe their marketing efforts.

College #1	College #2

Name ______________________________ Date __________ Class ____________________

Lesson 5.1 Understand the Need for Marketing Information

LESSON QUIZ

Directions For each of the following statements, if the statement is true, write a T on the answer line; if the statement is false, write an F on the answer line.

_____ 1. Competition is becoming less intense for most businesses.

_____ 2. To become more competitive, a business needs to understand the strengths and weaknesses of its competition.

_____ 3. Customers' needs generally remain the same over time.

_____ 4. Because most consumers are able to satisfy their basic needs, they devote more of their resources to satisfying their wants.

_____ 5. Effective marketing information improves decisions made by businesses.

_____ 6. Businesses that understand their customers' wants and needs in their home country will be able to use the same marketing strategies in international markets.

_____ 7. Effective marketing information reduces the risk of decision making.

Directions For each of the following items, decide which choice best completes the statement. Write the letter that identifies your choice on the answer line.

_____ 8. __________ purchases are not essential, so consumers can decide whether or not to purchase them.
A. Unwanted
B. Secondary
C. Luxury
D. Discretionary

_____ 9. Important factors facing businesses today that increase the need to gather and study information include all of the following except
A. consumer differences
B. expanding choices
C. larger marketing budgets
D. more intense competition

_____10. To make effective marketing decisions, marketers need information about
A. consumers
B. the business environment
C. the marketing mix
D. all of the above

Activity 1 • Cars, Cars, Cars

Directions Assume you are a car dealer who has been in business for many years. Your dealership has emphasized the sale of luxury, high-priced new cars, so most sales have been to middle-aged, upper-income buyers. Within the past year your manufacturer has introduced a new line of moderately priced, sportier, fuel-efficient cars. As a result, a younger group of customers is coming into your dealership who have different needs and wants related to auto purchases. You want to serve this market segment but need to understand it better.

1. Do you believe all of the new customers will be in the same target market? Why or why not?

____

____

____

2. What information would be needed to determine if the new shoppers will be good prospective customers?

____

____

____

____

3. What important mix elements should be considered in attempting to reach this market?

____

____

____

____

Activity 2 • Successful Marketing in Your Community

Directions Select a business that has been successful in your neighborhood or community for many years. Identify the reasons for its success by describing three important characteristics for each of the information categories in the table below that apply to the business.

Consumers	Marketing Mix	Business Environment
1.	1.	1.
2.	2.	2.
3.	3.	3.

Name ______________________________ Date __________ Class ____________________

Lesson 5.2 Find and Manage Marketing Information

LESSON QUIZ

Directions For each of the following statements, if the statement is true, write a T on the answer line; if the statement is false, write an F on the answer line.

_____ 1. For most marketing decisions, there is usually only one good source of information.

_____ 2. Customer records and sales information are examples of external information.

_____ 3. A business must evaluate each source of information to determine if it meets the organization's needs in terms of accuracy, time, detail, and cost.

_____ 4. Marketing information can come from internal sources, external sources, and marketing research.

_____ 5. A customer club is an effective way for a business to gather information about its customers.

_____ 6. It is not legal for businesses to use information obtained from trade and professional associations.

_____ 7. Using a marketing information system (MkIS) will require more time to gather information than using marketing research.

_____ 8. An important characteristic of a storage system in an MkIS is that it must protect the data.

Directions For each of the following items, decide which choice best completes the statement. Write the letter that identifies your choice on the answer line.

_____ 9. Which of the following would not be an important source of information for marketers?
A. sales records
B. production reports
C. marketing performance information
D. all are important

_____10. An external source of information for marketers is
A. government records
B. sales records
C. financial statements
D. all of the above

_____11. One of the five elements of an effective information system includes
A. market research
B. analysis
C. results
D. marketing mix

Activity 1 • Information Scavenger Hunt

Directions Locate an information source that provides the following information. Record the answer and the information source.

1. What is the population of your community?

____

2. What is the average income of the residents in your community?

____

3. How many grocery stores are in your community?

____

4. What is the highest and lowest price charged for a gallon of gasoline in your community?

____

5. What is the name of the nearest minor league baseball team?

____

6. By what percentage has the population of your community changed in the past 10 years?

____

7. Which states are touched by the Great Lakes?

____

8. How many tablespoons are in a ¼ cup?

____

9. In the year 2005, which state had the smallest population?

____

10. Identify an important world event that happened on this date in history.

____

11. Where is the city of Timbuktu located?

____

12. What was the highest-rated TV show during the past week? How many viewers did it have?

____

Name ____ Date ____________ Class__________________________

Lesson 5.3 Use Marketing Research

LESSON QUIZ

Directions For each of the following statements, if the statement is true, write a T on the answer line; if the statement is false, write an F on the answer line.

_____ 1. Marketing research should be used when a business needs to solve a specific and unique problem.

_____ 2. The first step in marketing research is to complete a situation analysis.

_____ 3. Information already collected for another purpose that can be used to solve the current problem is secondary data.

_____ 4. The number of people in a sample is smaller than the number in a population.

_____ 5. The results of marketing research should be presented orally to decision makers rather than in a written report.

_____ 6. A marketing research report should describe the purpose of the study and the research procedures followed to collect the information.

_____ 7. In most cases, the marketing researchers completing the study do not make the final decisions about solutions.

_____ 8. Marketing research is usually too expensive and time-consuming to be a valuable tool for businesses.

Directions For each of the following items, decide which choice best completes the statement. Write the letter that identifies your choice on the answer line.

_____ 9. After reviewing the situation and the available information, a researcher
A. states the problem
B. asks others to review the problem statement
C. might be able to identify a solution without completing a research study
D. prepares the research report

_____10. Information collected for the first time to solve the problem being studied is ________ data.
A. biased
B. numerical
C. secondary
D. primary

_____11. A procedure in which everyone in the population has an equal chance of being selected in the sample is
A. a focus group
B. random sampling
C. marketing research
D. an experiment

Activity 1 • Use Research to Make a Decision

Directions Apply the principles of scientific problem solving to the decision in the following scenario. Describe how you would use the procedure and information to make a decision.

You are a senior in high school and need to save $5,000 for a used car you have selected. You have $2,500 in a college savings account. You have two job offers:

Children's toy store assistant manager

- Pay—$6.55/hour, $.50/hour extra for working the closing shift
- Hours—20 hours per week; you must work either Saturday or Sunday; and you must close at least one night per week, which involves staying until 10:30 P.M.

Wait staff at an upscale restaurant

- Pay—$2.50/hour plus tips
- Hours—15–25 hours per week, including both Friday and Saturday nights most weeks

Define the problem.

____

____

____

Analyze the situation.

____

____

____

Develop a data-collection procedure.

____

____

____

Gather and study information.

____

____

____

Propose a solution.

____

____

____

Name ______________________________ Date ____________ Class ____________

Lesson 5.4 Collect Primary Data

LESSON QUIZ

Directions For each of the following statements, if the statement is true, write a T on the answer line; if the statement is false, write an F on the answer line.

_____ 1. Open-ended questions are used when researchers are attempting to identify the problem or completing a situation analysis.

_____ 2. When possible, survey questions should be written in such a way that respondents are directed to one answer rather than the others.

_____ 3. The responses to a survey should be kept confidential.

_____ 4. When possible, surveys should collect more information than necessary in order to answer future questions.

_____ 5. An objective way for researchers to collect information is by observing the behavior of participants.

_____ 6. Experiments occur when researchers give two different forms of a survey to respondents.

_____ 7. Experiments are not used as often in marketing research as surveys or observations.

_____ 8. Test markets should be selected that reflect consumer and competitive characteristics important to the company.

Directions For each of the following items, decide which choice best completes the statement. Write the letter that identifies your choice on the answer line.

_____ 9. A planned set of questions to which individuals or groups of people respond is

A. a survey
B. random sampling
C. a marketing research report
D. an experiment

_____10. A focus group is

A. a group of marketers who develop a survey
B. a small number of people who meet to discuss an issue
C. a list of specific questions to be included in a survey
D. another name for a target market

_____11. Experiments operated in laboratories where researchers create the situation to be studied are known as

A. focus groups
B. test markets
C. simulations
D. random sampling

Activity 1 • Improve Airline Service

Directions The airline industry is very competitive and lately has experienced small profit margins. A major U.S. carrier decided to survey its passengers to determine their opinion of the quality of the airline's service. Surveys were mailed to 7,500 passengers who had flown on at least two trips in the past six months. Responses to the survey are shown in the table. Calculate the percentages for each response to complete the table and answer the questions that follow it.

Questions	Responses					
	Yes	%	No	%	No Answer	%
1. Was your flight on time?	3,429		1,221		0	
2. Were you able to board promptly?	3,275		1,375		0	
3. Was your luggage check-in handled efficiently?	4,406		39		205	
4. Were the following amenities offered to you during your flight?						
Magazines	4,013		637			
Pillow or blanket	2,543		2,107			
Headset	4,439		211			
Special request	1,589		386		2675	
5. Were the beverages and snacks served promptly?	3,979		671		0	
6. Were flight attendants pleasant and helpful?	3,261		889		500	
7. If applicable, did the airline personnel provide information regarding connecting flights?	2,341		267		2,042	
8. When given a choice of airlines, would you fly this airline again?	4,523		127		0	

1. What percentage of surveys was returned? ____________________

2. Visually illustrate the percentage results based on total respondents by constructing a pie chart or bar graph for each question. Color code the responses to make the graphs more visually appealing.

3. What are the current strengths, if any, of this airline's service?

____

____

____

4. What problem areas, if any, do you believe the airline should investigate further?

____

____

____

Name ______________________________ Date __________ Class ____________________

Lesson 6.1 Understand Consumer Behavior

LESSON QUIZ

Directions For each of the following statements, if the statement is true, write a T on the answer line; if the statement is false, write an F on the answer line.

_____ 1. To implement the marketing concept, a business must understand its customers.

_____ 2. A final consumer buys goods and services to produce and market other goods and services or for resale.

_____ 3. A need is an unfulfilled desire

_____ 4. According to Maslow's hierarchy of needs, you must satisfy your need for security before you can satisfy any of the others.

_____ 5. Meeting your physiological needs is optional.

_____ 6. Business consumers buy goods and services to resell or for use in producing and marketing other goods and services.

_____ 7. Consumers are at different levels on the hierarchy of needs.

_____ 8. There are seven levels in the hierarchy of needs.

Directions For each of the following items, decide which choice best completes the statement. Write the letter that identifies your choice on the answer line.

_____ 9. Which of the following is a part of consumer behavior?
A. how a competitor prices its products
B. the design of a marketing research study
C. factors that influence how people purchase and use products and services
D. all are correct

_____10. A final consumer might purchase a product for all of the following reasons except
A. for personal use
B. at the request of family members
C. to use for a hobby or personal interest
D. for use in a part-time business

_____11. The first (bottom) level in the hierarchy of needs is
A. security
B. esteem
C. social
D. physiological

_____12. Gaining respect and recognition from others satisfies
A. security needs
B. esteem needs
C. self-actualization needs
D. all of the above

Activity 1 • Maslow's Hierarchy of Needs

Directions Place the listed items on the correct level of Maslow's hierarchy of needs, matching each item to the type of need it satisfies.

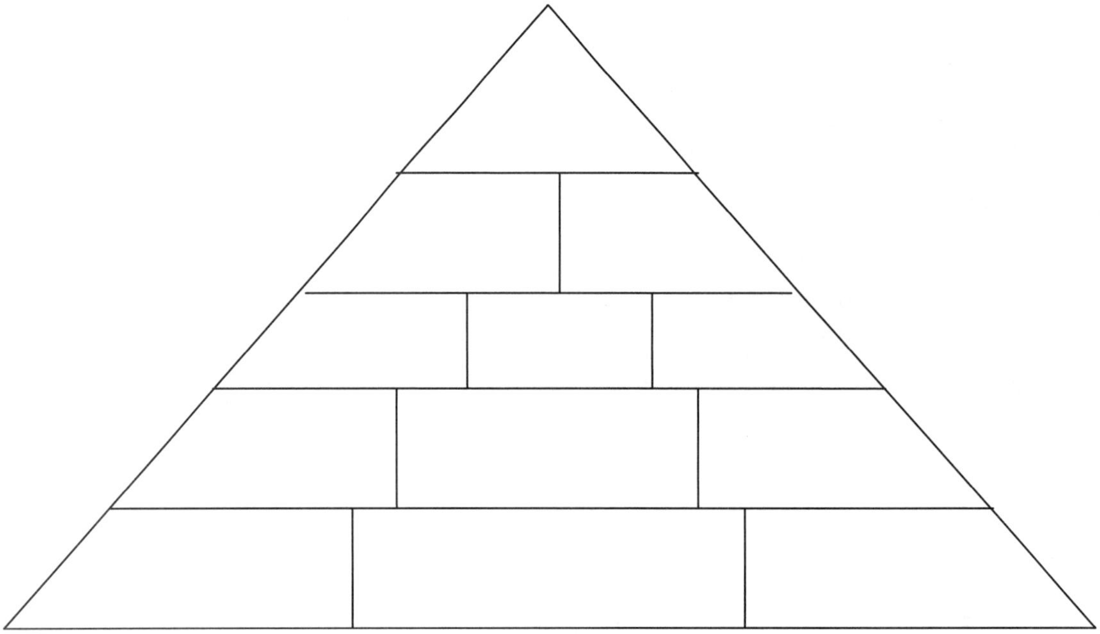

Buy a luxury car	Join an athletic team	Invest in a retirement plan
Attend a wedding	Buy car insurance	Order a pizza
Take medicine for an illness	Write a novel	Apply for a job
Go dancing	Become more physically fit	Heat your house in the winter

Activity 2 • How Is It Used?

Directions Identify a specific use for each of the items listed below and determine if the purchaser would be a final consumer or a business consumer.

Product	Product Use	Consumer Type
1. Diamond	______________________	______________________
2. Furniture polish	______________________	______________________
3. Textbook	______________________	______________________
4. Potatoes	______________________	______________________
5. Light bulb	______________________	______________________
6. Desk chair	______________________	______________________

Name ______________________________________ Date ___________ Class______________________

Lesson 6.2 What Motivates Buyers?

LESSON QUIZ

Directions For each of the following statements, if the statement is true, write a T on the answer line; if the statement is false, write an F on the answer line.

_____ 1. Advertisers can use fear effectively to motivate customers to buy some products and services.

_____ 2. Businesses have discovered that emotional motives are not very strong and seldom influence consumer behavior.

_____ 3. Loyalty is a rational motive.

_____ 4. Business consumers may base purchase decisions on patronage motives.

_____ 5. Consumers follow a series of six steps when making a purchase decision.

_____ 6. The first step in making a decision is recognizing a need, desire, or problem.

_____ 7. Businesses that pay attention to post-purchase behavior are more likely to develop loyal customers.

Directions For each of the following items, decide which choice best completes the statement. Write the letter that identifies your choice on the answer line.

_____ 8. Reasons to purchase based on feelings, beliefs, or attitudes are
A. hedonic motives
B. rational motives
C. patronage motives
D. ethical motives

_____ 9. If you shop in the same store time after time, your motivation for choosing the business is
A. hedonic
B. rational
C. patronage
D. repetitive

_____10. An important part in the first step of the consumer decision-making process is
A. gathering information about alternative solutions
B. determining if you have adequate information to make a decision
C. determining the strength of the need and the urgency to satisfy the need
D. realizing whether a product provides a solution to a problem

_____11. Consumers evaluate their satisfaction with a product
A. just before they purchase the product
B. when they compare alternative products
C. when the need is recognized
D. after they purchase the product

Activity 1 • Culture Change

Directions Using resources from your school or public library and interviews with older family members or friends, research important changes in our culture that have occurred in the past 50 years. Choose at least six cultural changes that have occurred and determine how marketers have responded to these changes with new or improved products or services. You may want to focus your study on a specific cultural group.

1. ______________________________

   Response: ______________________________

2. ______________________________

   Response: ______________________________

3. ______________________________

   Response: ______________________________

4. ______________________________

   Response: ______________________________

5. ______________________________

   Response: ______________________________

6. ______________________________

   Response: ______________________________

Name ______________________________ Date __________ Class ____________________

Lesson 6.3 Influence Consumer Decisions

LESSON QUIZ

Directions For each of the following statements, if the statement is true, write a T on the answer line; if the statement is false, write an F on the answer line.

_____ 1. Personal identity consists of the characteristics that make a person unique.

_____ 2. Personality is the way a person lives as reflected by material goods, activities, and relationships.

_____ 3. Because people are healthier and living longer, a person's age no longer has much influence on consumer behavior.

_____ 4. Your school is a part of your social environment.

_____ 5. Marketing based on appealing to an important reference group of a target market is usually effective.

_____ 6. The three types of decision making are routine, extensive, and continuous.

_____ 7. Marketers generally do not believe gender to be a key influence on buying decisions.

Directions For each of the following items, decide which choice best completes the statement. Write the letter that identifies your choice on the answer line.

_____ 8. The history, beliefs, customs, and traditions of a group that are passed on from generation to generation is the group's
A. personality characteristics
B. culture
C. social class
D. reference group

_____ 9. Your reference group has an important influence on
A. the money you have available for purchases
B. where you live
C. much of your behavior and image
D. all of the above

_____10. When consumers methodically go through all of the steps in decision making, they are using
A. limited decision making
B. routine decision making
C. extensive decision making
D. objective decision making

_____11. The appropriate role of marketers in consumer decision making is to
A. match their products and services to the needs and expectations of customers
B. use promotion to change consumer decision making
C. assume that all consumers use extensive decision making
D. find consumers who are brand loyal

Activity 1 • Political Marketing

Directions As the media specialist for a presidential candidate, your research indicates that many people base their choice of candidates on emotional reasons. In this election, the economy is weak and many people are worried about their jobs and income. In addition, people want a president they can trust and who is an effective communicator. Based on this information, what advice would you give to your candidate about buying (voting) motives and how to use the steps in the decision-making process to win the election?

Buying motives:____

____

____

DECISION-MAKING PROCESS

Need recognition: ____

____

Information search:____

____

Alternative evaluation:_______________________________________

____

Purchase: ____

____

Postpurchase evaluation: _____________________________________

____

Activity 2 • Types of Decisions

Directions Classify the following products as either requiring routine, limited, or extensive decision making and indicate a reason why you made the selection.

1. Light bulbs: ____

   Reason:____

   ____

2. Financial planning services:________________________________

   Reason:____

   ____

3. Rental car:____

   Reason: ____

   ____

Name ______________________________ Date __________ Class ______________________

Lesson 7.1 Focus on Market Segments

LESSON QUIZ

Directions For each of the following statements, if the statement is true, write a T on the answer line; if the statement is false, write an F on the answer line.

_____ 1. Each person is a part of only one market segment that influences all of his or her purchase decisions.

_____ 2. Businesses use marketing information and market research to complete market segmentation.

_____ 3. Dividing consumers into markets based on where they live is referred to as demographic segmentation.

_____ 4. Market segmentation does not apply to business markets.

_____ 5. A market opportunity is an identified market with excellent potential based on careful research.

_____ 6. Target markets should be selected from the segments that have the greatest potential.

_____ 7. A successful company's market share should be larger than the market potential.

Directions For each of the following items, decide which choice best completes the statement. Write the letter that identifies your choice on the answer line.

_____ 8. __________ directs a company's marketing mix at a large and heterogeneous group of consumers.
A. Mass marketing
B. Advertising
C. Market segmentation
D. Market research

_____ 9. People's interests and values are referred to as
A. demographics
B. psychographics
C. needs and wants
D. personal qualities

_____10. An identified market with excellent potential based on careful research is a
A. market opportunity
B. target market
C. market segment
D. mass market

_____11. If the market potential for gasoline sales in one community is $10,385,990 and one convenience store has a market share of 8%, the value of its gasoline sales is
A. $8,308,792
B. $11,216,869
C. $83,087,920
D. $830,879.20

Activity 1 • Appeal to Segments

Directions Billboards are an effective means of catching the attention of passers-by with a short, focused message. Select a product that you believe will appeal to a market segment that includes people driving to and from your school. In the space below, design a billboard with a creative, attention-getting message that will appeal specifically to that market segment. Explain your decision by answering the questions below the billboard.

Explain your decisions:

What is the target market?

____

____

What are the important characteristics of the market segment?

____

____

Why do you believe the billboard will appeal to the market segment you selected?

____

____

Name ______________________________ Date __________ Class ______________

Lesson 7.2 Position for Competitive Advantage

LESSON QUIZ

Directions For each of the following statements, if the statement is true, write a T on the answer line; if the statement is false, write an F on the answer line.

_____ 1. Positioning highlights differences between competitors in the mind of the consumer.

_____ 2. One method of positioning a product is to associate a type of user with the product.

_____ 3. Once consumers have developed a perception of a product, businesses will be unable to change the product's position.

_____ 4. Anytime you see an ad comparing one product with a well-known competitor's products, you can assume that a competitor positioning strategy is being used.

_____ 5. Consumer perceptions are the images consumers have of competing goods and services in the marketplace.

_____ 6. Successful companies base their positioning strategy decisions solely on the actions of their competitors.

_____ 7. Changes in the business environment can have an impact on the success of a company's positioning strategy.

Directions For each of the following items, decide which choice best completes the statement. Write the letter that identifies your choice on the answer line.

_____ 8. Which of the following is not a basis for product positioning?
A. price and quality
B. use or application
C. product attribute
D. brand name

_____ 9. A business will do well when consumers perceive the attributes of its product as being
A. expensive
B. close to the consumers' ideal image
C. cheap
D. of average quality

_____10. The ideal competitive position for a product is when consumers view the company's product attributes as ______________ when compared to those of competitors.
A. superior
B. cheaper
C. different
D. similar

_____11. The business environment includes
A. resource availability
B. changing consumer needs
C. new technology
D. all of the above

Activity 1 • Marketing Positions

Directions Marketers work very hard on positioning their products, services, and businesses. They continually strive to create a special image to set themselves apart from everyone else.

You carry these images in your mind without consciously thinking of them. In column 1 of the chart, write a specific product or business you are familiar with that belongs to the general product category. In column 2, write your view of the specific positioning image of that product or business. In column 3, identify the basis for positioning you believe the marketer used to create that image in your mind. Select one of the six categories discussed in the lesson.

The first item is completed for you as an example. The last three general product categories are blank. In these blank spaces, identify product categories you believe have companies with effective positioning strategies and complete each column to describe a specific example.

General Product Category	Specific Product or Business	Image	Basis for Positioning and Image
Video game console	Nintendo Wii	Bringing an active gaming experience to more people	Product user
Automobile			
Perfume or cologne			
Cell phone			
Restaurant			
Specialty clothing store			
Cable TV channel			

Name ______________________ Date __________ Class ______________

Lesson 7.3 Compete for Market Segments

LESSON QUIZ

Directions For each of the following statements, if the statement is true, write a T on the answer line; if the statement is false, write an F on the answer line.

_____ 1. The type of competition a business faces will affect its positioning.

_____ 2. An example of direct competition is Nike and Reebok.

_____ 3. Indirect competition occurs when two brands of similar products are compared.

_____ 4. All businesses should avoid using price competition.

_____ 5. Emphasizing qualities such as service, quality, credit, location, guarantees, or a unique image is appropriate for businesses using non-price competition.

_____ 6. Businesses that indirectly compete with each other will need to use non-price competition.

_____ 7. Competition forces businesses to offer reasonable prices for the products and services that consumers use.

_____ 8. Competition limits the variety of products that are available to consumers.

Directions For each of the following items, decide which choice best completes the statement. Write the letter that identifies your choice on the answer line.

_____ 9. Rivalry among firms on the basis of price and value is called
A. direct competition
B. indirect competition
C. price competition
D. all of the above

_____10. Every company wants to make its products
A. more expensive
B. distinctive
C. less expensive
D. as similar as possible to the competition

_____11. Competition creates products that
A. are improvements over existing products
B. are reasonably priced
C. offer new product ideas
D. all of the above

_____12. Which of these is not a benefit of competition?
A. It allows businesses to charge higher prices for products.
B. It forces businesses to offer reasonable prices to customers.
C. It encourages businesses to improve their products.
D. It encourages business to search for new product ideas.

Activity 1 • Learn about Your Competition—Pricing Strategies

Directions Each business has its own pricing strategy based on its marketing mix. For each of the following products or services, determine the price five different businesses charge by visiting the store, reading advertisements, or using the Internet. Use stores in your own community or a close larger city if possible. Write the name of the business in the upper cell and write the price that business charges in the lower cell for each item.

	Business/Price #1	Business/Price #2	Business/Price #3	Business/Price #4	Business/Price #5
Child's haircut					
One dozen bagels					
New movie rental					
Oil change for a car					
Digital camera					

Directions Select the product or service showing the greatest price differences and illustrate your findings with a bar graph. Make sure you identify each price and business in your graph.

Name ______________________________________ Date __________ Class ____________________

Lesson 7.4 Learn about the Competition

LESSON QUIZ

Directions For each of the following statements, if the statement is true, write a T on the answer line; if the statement is false, write an F on the answer line.

_____ 1. If a company has a marketing mix that meets the needs of its customers, it will not need to gather information on the marketing mixes its competitors use.

_____ 2. If a company lowers its prices, all companies in direct competition will have to lower their prices as well.

_____ 3. Making a product available to consumers in more locations will usually add to the business's costs.

_____ 4. If customers prefer the new product of a competitor, it will be difficult to win those customers back.

_____ 5. An advantage of promotional strategies is that they can be changed quickly.

_____ 6. The process of gaining competitive market information is called market intelligence.

_____ 7. Because it is difficult to determine the source of much of the information on the Internet, it is not a good source of competitive information.

_____ 8. It would be unethical to obtain and use information that a competitor considers to be private and does not disclose outside of the organization.

Directions For each of the following items, decide which choice best completes the statement. Write the letter that identifies your choice on the answer line.

_____ 9. Making changes in the distribution strategy should be planned carefully because
A. it usually takes a great deal of time
B. it often involves other businesses to implement the change
C. it can increase the price customers must pay for the product
D. all are correct

_____10. The competitive marketing mix element that usually receives more attention than others in the mix is
A. product
B. distribution
C. price
D. promotion

_____11. Appropriate methods to gain competitive information would include all of the following except
A. purchasing and analyzing competitors' products
B. attending trade shows
C. asking the employees of competitors to share information
D. all are appropriate

Activity 1 • Competition and the Marketing Mix

Directions Businesses often emphasize a particular mix element when appealing to customers to differentiate themselves from their competitors. They believe that mix element provides the best competitive position for their business, product, or service.

For this project, identify nine businesses in your community. Study their advertising and identify which marketing mix element they emphasize to differentiate themselves from their competitors and appeal to their target market. In the table below, record the name of the business, the product or service it offers, and the marketing mix element it emphasizes. Make sure that your list includes examples for each of the four marketing mix elements.

Business Name	Product/Service	Marketing Mix Emphasis
1.		
2.		
3.		
4.		
5.		
6.		
7.		
8.		
9.		

Activity 2 • Gather Market Intelligence

Directions You are responsible for gathering market intelligence for a national retailer that specializes in educational games and toys. Use the Internet to identify a specific information source for each of the following market intelligence categories.

1. Trade show

____

2. Professional or trade association

____

3. Professional publication

____

4. Internet website

____

Name ________________________________ Date __________ Class ________________

Lesson 8.1 Technology, the Internet, and E-Commerce

LESSON QUIZ

Directions For each of the following statements, if the statement is true, write a T on the answer line; if the statement is false, write an F on the answer line.

_____ 1. Technology is the practical application of scientific knowledge.

_____ 2. The advanced procedures, techniques, and tools that replace physical labor are known as basic technology.

_____ 3. Many traditional businesses use the Internet to complete business activities.

_____ 4. E-commerce includes all the activities involved in selling goods over the Internet.

_____ 5. Brick-and-click businesses are those that complete almost all of their activities via retail stores, offices, or the factories where their products are manufactured.

_____ 6. A major advantage of doing business on the Internet is that companies have immediate access to prospective customers all over the world.

_____ 7. Businesses engaged in e-commerce do not need to use the marketing concept because they rarely, if ever, meet their customers.

Directions For each of the following items, decide which choice best completes the statement. Write the letter that identifies your choice on the answer line.

_____ 8. As of 2014, the Internet is used worldwide by approximately
A. 280 million people
B. 400 million people
C. 1 billion people
D. 3 billion people

_____ 9. A business that performs almost all of its business activities through the Internet is referred to as a
A. click-only business
B. brick-and-click business
C. brick-and-mortar business
D. electronic business

_____10. One of the disadvantages of using the Internet to conduct business is that
A. it allows products to be delivered directly to your computer
B. it makes the provision of customer service much less complicated
C. it changes the nature of competition
D. all of the above

_____11. Which element of the marketing mix is important to businesses using e-commerce?
A. product
B. price
C. distribution
D. All marketing mix elements are important.

Activity 1 • Business Information

Directions The Internet is an excellent source of information about businesses, regardless of whether or not they operate on the Internet. Sometimes, you will find information on a website created by the company. Other times, you will find information about a specific company on a website created by other businesses. These businesses may provide information for potential investors or customers. For the companies listed below, identify a website other than the company's own site that provides information about the company. Describe the information you found about the business, its products, or its history.

1. Burger King – website address:______________________________

2. LensCrafters – website address:______________________________

3. John Deere – website address:______________________________

4. American Express – website address:______________________________

Activity 2 • Identify and Analyze Websites

Directions Visit the websites for the five companies listed. Identify the Internet address (URL) for the business, describe a few features of the site, and identify the role or roles that each play in the company's marketing mix. Use additional sheets of paper to complete this activity.

Business	Internet Address (URL)	Website Features	Marketing Mix Role
Papa Johns	www.papajohns.com		
PBS Kids	www.pbskids.org		
iTunes	www.apple.com/itunes		
PepsiCo	www.pepsico.com		
NetJets	www.netjets.com		

Name ____ Date ____________ Class__________________________

Lesson 8.2 The Emergence of Social Media

LESSON QUIZ

Directions For each of the following statements, if the statement is true, write a T on the answer line; if the statement is false, write an F on the answer line.

_____ 1. Social media enables open communication with groups of people.

_____ 2. The telephone is an early form of social media.

_____ 3. The process of emailing began as a military and research tool in the 1950s.

_____ 4. Social media is a powerful form of word-of-mouth communication.

_____ 5. Posting very short album reviews on Pinterest is considered micro-blogging.

_____ 6. Social media helps consumers build a community, making it more difficult for businesses to spread their message to those consumers.

_____ 7. Social media allows marketers to have full control over the messages they produce.

Directions For each of the following items, decide which choice best completes the statement. Write the letter that identifies your choice on the answer line.

_____ 8. All of the following are early applications of social media except
A. personal websites on Geocities
B. personal profiles on Sixdegrees.com
C. purchasing music through iTunes
D. file-sharing on Napster

_____ 9. Crowd-sourcing, an activity where a large number of people contribute their knowledge about a particular topic or phenomenon, is most closely associated with
A. social networks
B. collaboration
C. content communities
D. entertainment

_____10. It is important for business to have a well thought-out approach to social media because
A. marketers have no control over the conversations after the message is delivered
B. bad reviews by customers can quickly undo the efforts paid for by marketers
C. social media distributes power more evenly between marketer and consumer
D. all of the above

_____11. Because marketers are able to talk with their audience through various social networks, social media promotes
A. community
B. trust
C. dialogue
D. sharing

Activity 1 • Marketing with Social Media

Directions Social media sites often have different purposes as well as different means for engaging consumers into the marketing discussion. In the chart below, you will see a listing of a variety of social media sites. Provide a description of each site and how marketers can use it to engage existing and potential customers into the conversation. Also, find information about the estimated number of unique visitors these sites receive each month. Finally, discuss why you think each social media site will be effective or not effective for marketers to use.

Social Media	Description (Include Type)	Customer Engagement	Estimated Monthly Visitors	Effective or Not
Facebook				
MySpace				
Twitter				
LinkedIn				
Bebo				
Friendster				
Meetup				
Flixster				
Tagged				
Pinterest				
Ning				
Flikr				
Classmates				
Vine				
Tumbler				
Ask.fm				
Wookiepedia				
Yelp				

Name ______________________ Date ____________ Class ______________

Lesson 8.3 Social Media as a Marketing Tool

LESSON QUIZ

Directions For each of the following statements, if the statement is true, write a T on the answer line; if the statement is false, write an F on the answer line.

_____ 1. Social media sites have a lot in common with the earliest marketplaces.

_____ 2. Immediacy is related to the ability of consumers to communicate with marketers as well as with each other in real time.

_____ 3. There is no advantage for politicians who wish to utilize social media as a powerful communication tool.

_____ 4. Trending refers to a topic or discussion that is currently popular in social media or other Web-based formats.

_____ 5. If the idea of social media is to develop interactions with consumers, then marketers need to focus on communicating with large groups of people in a somewhat anonymous fashion.

_____ 6. Marketplaces of all shapes and sizes are an important place for people to connect with each other.

_____ 7. Marketers of popular brands should keep track of their Wikipedia pages and correct any and all information that consumers get wrong.

Directions For each of the following items, decide which choice best completes the statement. Write the letter that identifies your choice on the answer line.

_____ 8. In traditional marketplaces as well as social media, one of the major characteristics is that merchants can speak with customers and customers can provide feedback. This promotes the ________ nature of the marketplace.

A. personal and interactive
B. immediate
C. word-of-mouth
D. connective

_____ 9. To be successful in adapting social media to the needs of the business, marketers should

A. have a series of small interactions with customers
B. develop a social media mindset
C. focus on the content of social media
D. all of the above

_____10. YouTube does an excellent job of providing a space for

A. sharing information
B. collaboration
C. trending
D. user-generated content

Activity 1 • Internet Advertisements

Directions The consumers who choose to visit a particular social media site can be placed in a market segment. Based on this segmentation, advertisers will choose to place advertisements on sites that attract the same market segment they have chosen. Visit three social media sites you normally visit. Record the advertisers on the site, describe the market segment, and explain why the advertisers selected this site.

1. Website address:______________________ Segment: ______________________
   Advertiser:____
   Reason:____
   ____
   ____

2. Website address:______________________ Segment: ______________________
   Advertiser:____
   Reason:____
   ____
   ____

3. Website address: ______________________ Segment: ______________________
   Advertiser:____
   Reason:____
   ____
   ____

Activity 2 • Banner Advertisement

Directions Like traditional advertisements, Internet ads are designed to attract a specific market segment that will be interested in their products, even when those ads are used on social media sites. Identify a product and market segment. On a separate sheet of paper, draw an Internet banner advertisement that would attract the selected consumers and explain your choices in the design.

Product:______________________ Segment:______________________

Reason:____

____

____

____

____

____

____

Name ______________________________ Date __________ Class ____________________

Lesson 9.1 Elements of a Marketing Strategy

LESSON QUIZ

Directions For each of the following statements, if the statement is true, write a T on the answer line; if the statement is false, write an F on the answer line.

_____ 1. A marketing strategy is the way marketing activities are planned and coordinated to achieve an organization's goals.

_____ 2. Effective marketers try to serve all potential consumers in a market.

_____ 3. The starting point and most important factor used to segment a market are the demographic characteristics of consumers.

_____ 4. A segment represents components of a market in which people have one or more similar characteristics.

_____ 5. A business should never target more than one segment in a market.

_____ 6. A target market is a clearly identified segment of the market to which a business wishes to appeal.

_____ 7. Each target market requires a unique marketing mix that responds to the differences among the target markets.

Directions For each of the following items, decide which choice best completes the statement. Write the letter that identifies your choice on the answer line.

_____ 8. Which of the following factors would not be used to segment a market?
A. demographics
B. psychographics
C. buying behavior
D. intensity of competition

_____ 9. An effective target market must be composed of
A. a large number of potential customers
B. people who already prefer the businesses products and services
C. individuals with common, important needs that are different from those outside the target market
D. all of the above

_____10. Each target market requires a marketing mix that
A. differs in important ways from other target markets
B. emphasizes product features rather than price and promotion
C. is based on the needs of the business
D. is completely different from that offered by major competitors

_____11. Which of these is not a behavioral segmentation factor?
A. consumer's previous experience with product
B. age, income, and education level of consumer
C. whether the decision is rational or emotional
D. amount of time the consumer takes to gather and evaluate produt information

Activity 1 • Segment Your Class

Directions Using your classroom as a sample, survey your classmates and divide the market, consisting of the entire class, into smaller segments using the criteria listed below. Describe each segment.

1. Based on demographic characteristics such as age, gender, race/ethnicity, and year in school: Number of segments:________________________________

Segment 1	Segment 2	Segment 3	Segment 4

2. Based on psychographic characteristics such as the type of music, sports, and leisure activities they enjoy: Number of segments:________________________________

Segment 1	Segment 2	Segment 3	Segment 4

3. Based on attitudes about school such as importance of grades, time spent studying, and the value of post-secondary education: Number of segments:________________________________

Segment 1	Segment 2	Segment 3	Segment 4

4. Using an additional sheet of paper, prepare a graph identifying the specific segments and the number of students for each of the segmenting categories studied above.

Activity 2 • Sell to a Segment

Directions Choose a target market from the market segments described in Activity 1 and identify a product or service you would market to it. Describe why the product and target segment fit together.

Target Segment:________________________________ Product:____________________________

Reasons for your choices: ____

____

____

Name ______________________________ Date __________ Class ______________

Lesson 9.2 Marketing Mix Alternatives

LESSON QUIZ

Directions For each of the following statements, if the statement is true, write a T on the answer line; if the statement is false, write an F on the answer line.

_____ 1. It is easiest for businesses to compete when their products are nearly identical to those of their competitors.

_____ 2. The product or service as a marketing mix element includes anything the business offers to the customer that will be used to satisfy needs.

_____ 3. Features can be added to a basic product to make one company's product different from and better than competitors' products.

_____ 4. Options give customers choices of the product features they want to purchase.

_____ 5. A product's brand name is never an important factor when customers make a decision to buy.

_____ 6. In addition to the type of transportation to use, distribution decisions include order processing, inventory control, product handling, protective packaging, and customer service.

_____ 7. Promotion is very important in the maturity stage of a product's life cycle.

_____ 8. A product faces its greatest competition during the growth stage of the life cycle.

Directions For each of the following items, decide which choice best completes the statement. Write the letter that identifies your choice on the answer line.

_____ 9. Products aimed at a large market tend to be very
A. similar
B. unique
C. expensive
D. inexpensive

_____10. When customers see few differences between products, they are more likely to choose a product based on
A. quality
B. brand name
C. price
D. convenience

_____11. In which stage of the product life cycle do profits in the market start to go down?
A. introduction
B. growth
C. decline
D. maturity

Activity 1 • Improve Market Appeal

Directions Examine two products you have purchased and used—one that you found to meet your needs very well and one that was less satisfying than you expected. In the chart below, describe each part of the product element of the marketing mix, what made it satisfying, and what you would recommend as an improvement. Identify how each of the other marketing mix elements influenced your decision to buy and contributed to your satisfaction.

Product 1 (very satisfying)	Basic Product	Features/Options
	Services	Brand/Image
	Packaging	Guarantee
	Uses	Price
	Distribution	Promotion
Product 2 (less satisfying)	Basic Product	Features/Options
	Services	Brand/Image
	Packaging	Guarantee
	Uses	Price
	Distribution	Promotion

Name ______________________________ Date __________ Class ______________

Lesson 9.3 Consumer Purchase Classifications

LESSON QUIZ

Directions For each of the following statements, if the statement is true, write a T on the answer line; if the statement is false, write an F on the answer line.

_____ 1. Generally consumers make all of their product and service purchases in the same way.

_____ 2. Consumers actively search for impulse goods.

_____ 3. Price is the most important factor when purchasing all types of shopping goods.

_____ 4. Most of the purchases consumers make in grocery stores are convenience goods.

_____ 5. Toothpaste may be a specialty good for some consumers.

_____ 6. Shopping goods are generally less expensive that convenience goods.

_____ 7. Consumers do not actively shop for emergency goods.

Directions For each of the following items, decide which choice best completes the statement. Write the letter that identifies your choice on the answer line.

_____ 8. Products or services that are purchased as a result of an urgent need are
A. staple goods
B. impulse goods
C. emergency goods
D. shopping goods

_____ 9. An example of an impulse good is
A. expensive jewelry
B. a bicycle
C. a piano
D. candy

_____10. For price-based shopping goods,
A. the product is the most important mix element
B. consumers see important differences in product features
C. customers expect to find price differences among brands
D. all are correct

_____11. Specialty goods
A. are always expensive
B. inspire strong brand loyalty
C. are not items a consumer actively shops to purchase
D. must be unique, high-quality products

Activity 1 • Classify Consumer Purchases

Directions Using the definitions of the categories, indicate a product/service for each classification based on your purchase behavior and the brand name you would prefer.

Classification	Product/Service Choice	Preferred Brand
Convenience staple goods	____________________	____________________
Convenience impulse goods	____________________	____________________
Convenience emergency goods	____________________	____________________
Attribute-based shopping goods	____________________	____________________
Price-based shopping goods	____________________	____________________
Unsought goods	____________________	____________________

Directions After you complete your list, compare it with the lists of several other classmates and answer the following questions.

Are the types of products in your lists more different or more alike? ____________________

____

____

____

What types of products were listed in different classifications by each of you? Why did that happen?

____

____

____

Are brand names more important in some classifications than in others? Are they more important to some students than to others in all categories? Explain your answer.__________

____

____

____

Do you have similar or different brand preferences? Why or why not? __________________

____

____

____

Name ______________________________ Date __________ Class ____________________

Lesson 9.4 Marketing Planning

LESSON QUIZ

Directions For each of the following statements, if the statement is true, write a T on the answer line; if the statement is false, write an F on the answer line.

_____ 1. Marketing for most businesses has become quite simple, involving only a small number of activities.

_____ 2. An effective marketing plan for a business should always be written.

_____ 3. Marketing planning is easy to do, is inexpensive, and takes very little time to accomplish.

_____ 4. A marketing plan is developed for a specific time period, usually six months to one year.

_____ 5. All businesses use the same information for developing their marketing plans.

_____ 6. Marketing plans should be based on performance of competitors rather than the performance of the company.

_____ 7. Much of the information needed to develop a marketing plan should already exist in a company's marketing information system (MkIS).

Directions For each of the following items, decide which choice best completes the statement. Write the letter that identifies your choice on the answer line.

_____ 8. The effect of a marketing plan on a business is
- A. it actually reduces planning time
- B. it guarantees the business will make a profit
- C. it improves decision making
- D. it reduces marketing costs

_____ 9. A marketing plan is based on
- A. the company's marketing strategy
- B. competitors' marketing plans
- C. government laws and regulations
- D. customer feedback

_____10. Developing a marketing plan encourages the business to
- A. make changes in the products offered for sale
- B. put marketers in charge of important business decisions
- C. coordinate marketing efforts with other business activities
- D. all of the above

_____11. Marketing planning requires
- A. time
- B. information
- C. people who understand planning procedures
- D. all of the above

Activity 1 • Marketing Planning Needs Marketing Information

Directions A useful marketing plan begins with information. Explain how a marketing plan can use the environmental information gathered by a marketing information system. The first environmental factor has been analyzed as an example.

MARKETING PLAN SECTION	TYPE OF INFORMATION	HOW IT IS USED
Economy	GDP, unemployment rate, recession, recovery, discretionary income, salaries	Invest in new product? Raise prices? Buy new equipment/land? Hire new employees? Change marketing mix?
Laws & Regulations		
Costs		
Competition		
Technology		
Social Factors		

Activity 2 • Plan a Trip

Directions You are planning a vacation for your family. You will drive to the destination and stay for three days before driving home. Complete the following information to help you plan your vacation. Gather needed information using the Internet and a search engine.

Destination: ______________________ Why did you choose this destination? __________________

What would make this a successful vacation for your family? ______________________________

____

Total miles to drive: ____________ Cost of gasoline: _____________ Hotel expense: ____________

Cost of meals: ______________Cost of entertainment (list activities): _________________________

Additional expenses (list expenses): _________________________ Total cost of vacation: _______

Name ________________________________ Date __________ Class ____________________

Lesson 9.5 Develop a Marketing Plan

LESSON QUIZ

Directions For each of the following statements, if the statement is true, write a T on the answer line; if the statement is false, write an F on the answer line.

_____ 1. A mission statement identifies the nature of the business or reasons it exists.

_____ 2. A market analysis identifies a business's strengths and weaknesses and the opportunities and threats it faces.

_____ 3. A marketing plan should not include a competitive analysis.

_____ 4. A positioning statement is a complete description of the target market and marketing mix the company will use.

_____ 5. Because marketing is so complex, it is not possible to specify the marketing activities that need to be completed in the written marketing plan.

_____ 6. If more than one market is identified as a target market, each market must be offered the identical marketing mix.

_____ 7. Information collected in evaluating action plans is used to make improvements in marketing activities while the marketing plan is being implemented.

Directions For each of the following items, decide which choice best completes the statement. Write the letter that identifies your choice on the answer line.

_____ 8. A market analysis is often referred to as a __________ analysis.
A. SPAM
B. SWOT
C. AIDCA
D. EIEIO

_____ 9. An appropriate marketing goal would be to
A. increase market share by 5 percent in one year
B. improve the company's products
C. determine why the company is losing money
D. hire five new salespeople

_____10. The most important part of the marketing plan, in terms of the company's success, is
A. information gathered to create the marketing plan
B. development of a marketing strategy
C. input from the company's managers
D. evaluation of past performance

_____11. Which of the following questions would not be asked as part of the evaluation of marketing effectiveness?
A. Were marketing activities completed effectively and on time?
B. Were the marketing objectives accomplished?
C. Are the needs of the target market satisfied by the marketing mix?
D. All should be asked as part of the evaluation.

Activity 1 • Develop a Plan

Directions You currently work for a small neighborhood grocery store. Though the owner, Jay Knight, has operated the business successfully for 25 years, he does not know a great deal about marketing or developing a marketing plan. Recently, the business has faced increasing competition from a new convenience store one block away and a large supermarket located in a shopping center that is about two miles from the grocery store.

You believe that if the owner analyzed his business situation including the new competition, defined his target market, and made careful marketing mix decisions, the business could continue to be successful. You have asked if you could help develop a marketing plan.

1. Prepare a presentation to Jay Knight describing the parts of a marketing plan, its value to the business, and what would be needed to develop a plan for the grocery store.
2. Develop two charts or other visuals to support your presentation.
3. Be prepared to make your presentation to your teacher or to other students.

Activity 2 • Evaluate Results

Directions A marketing plan is useful only if the results can be evaluated. If they can't be evaluated, the business will not know what works and what does not work. Therefore, it is important that the mix elements can be measured. Read the following case and help the restaurant owner measure and analyze the results of the new marketing strategy.

The owner of an Italian restaurant was reviewing sales records and realized that sales were slow for dinner on Monday through Thursday. The restaurant seats 100 people. Records indicated that an average of 150 customers were served each night, and the average price of a dinner was $11. The owner decided that in order to increase sales, the restaurant would attempt to focus on a specific target market each day of the week. To support this, the following promotional campaign was developed with a supporting marketing mix to advertise special days: Monday, Kids Eat Free; Tuesday, 20% discount for Senior Citizens; Wednesday, Early Bird Special, 15% discount on all meals served before 6:00 p.m.; Thursday, Late Night Special, 15% discount on all meals served after 8:00 p.m.

1. Here are the results after the first week of the advertised specials. Calculate the average meal price each night based on gross sales.

Day	Customers	Gross Sales	Average Meal Price
Monday	350 customers (of which 105 were children)	$3,430	
Tuesday	190 customers (of which 95 were senior citizens)	1,919	
Wednesday	220 customers (of which 85 dined before 6:00)	2,464	
Thursday	260 customers (of which 130 dined after 8:00)	2,730	

2. Evaluate the effectiveness of each promotion and write a recommendation as to which should be continued. ______________________________

____

3. What additional information would be useful to the owner to plan a new marketing strategy?

____

____

____

____

Name ______________________________ Date __________ Class ____________________

Lesson 10.1 Start with a Product

LESSON QUIZ

Directions For each of the following statements, if the statement is true, write a T on the answer line; if the statement is false, write an F on the answer line.

_____ 1. Consumers have a different view of products than the businesses that produce them.

_____ 2. The satisfaction provided from a product's use is more important to consumers than its physical appearance.

_____ 3. Most consumer needs are so basic that businesspeople don't have to be concerned about them.

_____ 4. One of the markets that businesses understand very well is the teenage market.

_____ 5. If a product has been successful for a long time, it will probably remain successful because consumer needs seldom change.

_____ 6. Marketers can use feedback from salespeople to gain insight into both customers and competitors.

_____ 7. Market testing is an inexpensive, low-risk way to determine if a new product will be successful.

_____ 8. Marketers represent the consumer as products are designed and developed.

Directions For each of the following items, decide which choice best completes the statement. Write the letter that identifies your choice on the answer line.

_____ 9. To interest a consumer, a product must be
A. useful and meet the consumers' needs
B. physically attractive
C. low priced
D. all of the above

_____10. Consumer needs should be defined by
A. marketers
B. businesses
C. consumers
D. all of the above

_____11. A problem with using a test market for new products is
A. it is increasingly expensive
B. competitors are tipped off about a company's new marketing strategies
C. competitors will take actions to influence the test market results
D. all are correct

Activity 1 • Influence Purchase Decisions

Directions Complete the following table for five products by identifying the reasons most people buy that product and the features of the product you believe are most important in influencing consumers to choose a particular brand. When you have finished, compare your answers with those of other students to determine if you are generally agree or disagree.

Product	Reasons People Buy	Important Product Features
Energy drink		
Large-screen television		
College degree		
Sunglasses		
Movie tickets		

Activity 2 • Use Customer Ideas for Product Improvement

Directions Many ideas for product improvements come from discussions with customers. Interview three people. Interview three people, and discuss a product each one recently purchased that did not satisfy his or her needs or perform as well as expected. Ask questions about the product's design, features, and performance. Discuss the problems experienced with the product and why they occurred. Make several recommendations on how the product could be improved.

Product	Evaluation/Problems	Suggestions

Name ______________________________ Date __________ Class ____________________

Lesson 10.2 Components of the Product Mix

LESSON QUIZ

Directions For each of the following statements, if the statement is true, write a T on the answer line; if the statement is false, write an F on the answer line.

_____ 1. Offering a guarantee or testimonial is a way to differentiate products.

_____ 2. Businesses have many choices in the development of new products to make their brand unique.

_____ 3. In product design, the basic product is modified and improved with features and options.

_____ 4. The basic physical product must respond to an important customer need.

_____ 5. Every product enhancement will add to customer satisfaction.

_____ 6. A good way to improve customer satisfaction with products is to suggest the purchase of additional products that make the original product more useful.

_____ 7. A product package serves the dual purpose of promotion and protection.

Directions For each of the following items, decide which choice best completes the statement. Write the letter that identifies your choice on the answer line.

_____ 8. A group of similar products with slight variations in the product mix to satisfy different needs in a market is a
A. marketing mix
B. product line
C. product assortment
D. product category

_____ 9. Which of the following is not an important quality of a product's package?
A. ease of use
B. attractive
C. user safety
D. inexpensive

_____10. The legal protection of words or symbols for use by a company is a
A. trademark
B. brand name
C. logo
D. copyright

_____11. A(n) __________ includes additional options and features that allow a business to satisfy several target markets with one product.
A. basic product
B. enhanced product
C. extended product
D. optional product

Activity 1 • Product Components

Directions Select two products that people your age commonly purchase. The first product should cost less than $5, and the second, more than $50. Use the table below to identify three brands or variations of each product. Then list the differences among the three alternatives—features, options, uses, etc.

Product costing less than $5 ____________________________

Brand or Variation	Product Differences

Product costing more than $50 ______________________________

Brand or Variation	Product Differences

Activity 2 • Package Design

Directions In the space below or using a separate sheet of paper, design a package for a new men's fragrance named Pow! It will be sold in a 3-ounce glass bottle. The package should be attractive and attention-getting while providing necessary protection for the product.

Name ______________________ Date __________ Class ______________

Lesson 10.3 Products for Consumers and Businesses

LESSON QUIZ

Directions For each of the following statements, if the statement is true, write a T on the answer line; if the statement is false, write an F on the answer line.

_____ 1. Individuals or socially related groups who purchase products for personal consumption are known as consumer markets.

_____ 2. Businesses use the consumer purchase classification system to decide how to market their products in consumer markets.

_____ 3. Examples of capital equipment are tools, small machines, and furniture.

_____ 4. Most supplies are not uniquely developed for one business.

_____ 5. The price of raw materials influences the price charged for finished products.

_____ 6. Component parts have been either partially or totally processed by another company.

_____ 7. Operating equipment usually lasts longer than capital equipment.

_____ 8. Business markets make purchase decisions based on customer demand.

Directions For each of the following items, decide which choice best completes the statement. Write the letter that identifies your choice on the answer line.

_____ 9. Which of these is an example of a capital good?

A. small machine
B. office building
C. lumber
D. raw materials

_____10. The consumer purchase classification system is based on

A. the importance of the purchase to the consumer
B. the consumers' willingness to shop at different locations
C. the consumers' willingness to compare products before buying
D. all of the above

_____11. Which of these is not one of the categories in the business product classification system?

A. raw materials
B. supplies
C. unsought goods
D. component parts

_____12. Which of these is not an example of a raw material?

A. logs
B. oil
C. computer chip
D. grains

Activity 1 • Classifications

Directions Classifications provide a method of organizing a variety of products and other items. For example, books can be classified as fiction, nonfiction, mystery, romance, and autobiography. Identify several items that can be classified and list several categories into which the items can be organized.

Item **Classifications**

Activity 2 • New Business Planning

Directions New businesses are constantly being established. Each new business needs a variety of equipment and supplies. Select a new business. Identify one or more products the business will need to operate for each of the business product classifications.

Business Type: ______________________________

Purchases	Classification

Name ______________________________ Date __________ Class ____________________

Lesson 10.4 New Product Development

LESSON QUIZ

Directions For each of the following statements, if the statement is true, write a T on the answer line; if the statement is false, write an F on the answer line.

_____ 1. The Federal Trade Commission regulates how and when the word "new" can be used by businesses for their products.

_____ 2. Most businesses follow a similar series of steps to identify and develop new products.

_____ 3. Salespeople who work with customers every day are a good source of ideas for new products or product improvements.

_____ 4. The easiest step in new product development is usually finding ideas for new products.

_____ 5. Developing new product ideas should be done scientifically rather than using creative processes.

_____ 6. To avoid having too many new product ideas, companies should evaluate ideas in the initial idea development stage.

_____ 7. Companies should not be concerned about the financial analysis of a new product until after it is completely developed.

_____ 8. A prototype is used to test quality and costs before full-scale production begins.

Directions For each of the following items, decide which choice best completes the statement. Write the letter that identifies your choice on the answer line.

_____ 9. Good sources of new product ideas are
A. encyclopedias
B. newspapers
C. problems customers cannot solve with current products
D. all of the above

_____10. After determining that a product idea is feasible, the next step in product planning is to
A. perform a financial analysis
B. produce the product
C. identify a test market for the product
D. create and test a sample marketing strategy

_____11. The last step in product development is
A. product testing
B. full-scale introduction of the product into the market
C. financial analysis to determine profitability
D. asking consumers for their opinions of the new product

Activity 1 • Put Marketing Concepts Together

Directions Product planning does not occur in a vacuum. It is an integral function of marketing that is supported and combined with all other functions to make a business, product, or service successful. Referring to concepts and ideas you have studied in earlier chapters, describe how planning and developing a new product is affected by each of the following areas. To help you get started, the first answer is provided.

1. Marketing concept: *New product should respond to specific customer needs and create satisfying exchanges between the business and its customers. It should be viewed as a value by consumers and result in a profit for the business.*
2. Societal concerns: ____________________
3. Supply and demand: ____________________
4. Global marketplace: ____________________
5. Type of competition: ____________________
6. Existing products and markets: ____________________
7. Consumer decision making: ____________________
8. Marketing information and research: ____________________
9. Each marketing mix element: ____________________

Name ______________________________ Date __________ Class ____________________

Lesson 11.1 What Are Services?

LESSON QUIZ

Directions For each of the following statements, if the statement is true, write a T on the answer line; if the statement is false, write an F on the answer line.

_____ 1. Services are activities that are intangible.

_____ 2. The service industry is growing faster than the goods-producing industry.

_____ 3. Consumers spend a smaller percentage of their discretionary income on services and more on manufactured goods.

_____ 4. Competition from international businesses in manufacturing has led workers to seek jobs in the service sector of the U.S. economy.

_____ 5. Because people cannot physically touch a service, it is important for the marketer to focus on the benefits customers will receive from using the service.

_____ 6. A service is perishable in that it is produced and consumed at the same time.

_____ 7. Projections indicate that the fastest-growing service industry from 2012 to 2022 will be health care and social assistance.

Directions For each of the following items, decide which choice best completes the statement. Write the letter that identifies your choice on the answer line.

_____ 8. The goods-producing industry is
A. growing faster than the service industry
B. becoming more automated
C. hiring more employees as the industry grows
D. all of the above

_____ 9. A service is
A. produced and consumed in different locations
B. consumed at the same time it is produced
C. produced and then stored until it can be consumed
D. produced and consumed by the customer

_____10. Services are heterogeneous, meaning
A. they are consistent
B. they cost less than tangible goods
C. there are differences between services
D. they are similar, even when produced by different suppliers

_____11. Which of these is not a factor in the growth of employment in the service sector of the U.S. economy?
A. continuing economic expansion
B. automation in the goods-producing industry
C. complex products
D. lack of foreign competition

Activity 1 • Create an Image

Directions For each of the following services, locate a print, television, radio or Internet advertisement. Identify the target market the advertisement is directed at and the unique qualities and benefits stressed in the promotion of the service. Record your answers below.

1. Wireless telephone plan
   Target market: ______
   Promotional appeal: ______
2. Recreation or entertainment business
   Target Market: ______
   Promotional appeal: ______
3. Automobile insurance
   Target market: ______
   Promotional appeal: ______
4. Airline
   Target market: ______
   Promotional appeal: ______
5. Online education for a college or university
   Target market: ______
   Promotional appeal: ______

Activity 2 • Service Development

Directions You have decided to start a pet care business to take care of people's pets in their homes when they are out of town. Using the steps in new product development, outline the procedures you would go through to develop your service business.

Idea Development: ______

______

Idea Screening: ______

______

Strategy Development: ______

______

Product Development and Testing: ______

______

Product Marketing: ______

______

Name ______________________________ Date __________ Class ____________________

Lesson 11.2 Classify Services and Evaluate Quality

LESSON QUIZ

Directions For each of the following statements, if the statement is true, write a T on the answer line; if the statement is false, write an F on the answer line.

_____ 1. Services may be provided to businesses as well as to consumers.

_____ 2. Many not-for-profit organizations deliver services.

_____ 3. The amount of customer contact a service provider has is an effective way to classify services.

_____ 4. When categorizing services by the level of skill the provider possesses, services may be divided into professional and nonprofessional groups.

_____ 5. Service quality is defined by how comparable the quality of a company's service is to its main competitors.

_____ 6. Because services are intangible, it isn't possible to set measurable standards of performance.

_____ 7. One of the most important and useful indicators of customer satisfaction is repeat business.

Directions For each of the following items, decide which choice best completes the statement. Write the letter that identifies your choice on the answer line.

_____ 8. To develop a viable and appropriate marketing plan for a service, it is helpful for marketers to

A. plan the service before identifying the target market
B. recognize that each customer will need a different marketing plan
C. classify the service by type of consumers in the market, organizational goals, labor intensiveness, amount of customer contact, and skill level required
D. all of the above

_____ 9. The two types of markets for services are

A. profit and not-for-profit markets
B. business consumers and individual consumers
C. large and small businesses
D. retail and wholesale markets

_____10. Equipment-based services

A. are labor intensive
B. are tangible rather than intangible
C. require special attention to the distribution or location of the service
D. do not involve customer contact

Activity 1 • The Service Industry Continues to Change

Directions The service industry in the U.S. economy is growing faster than any other segment of the economy. In order to better understand this growth, research the topic in the library or on the Internet. Use the following questions as guides for your research, but add information as appropriate.

1. What are the major changes predicted in the service industry over the next 10 years?
2. What type of service jobs will increase and which will decrease in terms of numbers of employees needed? What is the demand for services in the global marketplace?
3. What social and economic changes are affecting the type and number of service businesses?
4. What new technologies are emerging that may affect the type of service businesses or the delivery of services?

Summarize your findings in the following space or on a separate sheet of paper.

Activity 2 • Service Evaluation

Directions Your older brother has started a mobile car washing and detailing service. Use the space below to design a form he can give to his customers so they can evaluate every aspect of the service he provides.

Name ______________________________ Date __________ Class ____________________

Lesson 11.3 Develop a Service Marketing Mix

LESSON QUIZ

Directions For each of the following statements, if the statement is true, write a T on the answer line; if the statement is false, write an F on the answer line.

_____ 1. Most services can be defined in terms of physical attributes.

_____ 2. Customers pay attention to tangible elements associated with the service.

_____ 3. Many services use endorsements as a promotional strategy.

_____ 4. Very few marketers believe that personal selling is a powerful promotional tool.

_____ 5. Promotional strategies should appeal to the buying motives of the target market by stressing the benefits customers will receive.

_____ 6. It is difficult for service businesses to change prices easily because the product is unique.

_____ 7. The distribution of services is primarily concerned with having the service in a location and at a time that are convenient for the consumer.

Directions For each of the following items, decide which choice best completes the statement. Write the letter that identifies your choice on the answer line.

_____ 8. To be effective, promotion of a service must
- A. be continuous
- B. create a mental image of the performance of the service and the benefits the customer will receive
- C. use publicity or word-of-mouth
- D. be very low cost

_____ 9. The price of a service
- A. can be easily changed by the business
- B. can be used to improve a business's market position and differentiate itself from competitors
- C. can be reduced by bundling several services
- D. all of the above

_____10. Distribution of a service
- A. cannot use intermediaries because it is perishable
- B. always requires a location that is convenient to the customer
- C. usually requires a short channel of distribution
- D. must be planned by the customer

_____10. The practice of combining several related services for one price is called
- A. bundling
- B. endorsing
- C. promoting
- D. packaging

Activity 1 • Plan Effective Day Care

Directions Many families have working parents and so need day-care services for their children. Develop a marketing strategy for a day-care center in your community that targets a specific group of consumers and that differs from existing day-care services. Be creative in the choices you make for product/service planning, pricing, promotion, and distribution but make sure they are consistent with effective services marketing. Be sure the decisions respond to the characteristics of the target market you identify.

Target Market: ____

____

____

Product/Service Management: ____

____

____

Pricing: ____

____

____

Distribution: ____

____

____

Promotion: ____

____

____

____

____

Activity 2 • Provide Computer Security

Directions You have heard many complaints from people who are upgrading to a new computer and want to sell, donate, or get rid of their older models. They are worried about the personal information and files that remain hidden on the hard drive. You have the software and skills needed to completely clean a hard drive, providing assurance to customers that they can safely dispose of the computers they no longer need. You want to start a part-time business. However, you need to let people know of your service. With this in mind, you have decided to create a one-page promotional flyer that you can distribute throughout the community.

Select the attributes of the service you want to promote. Design an attention-getting, persuasive advertisement. Include both text and graphics to convey the unique qualities and value of your service. Make sure the important elements of your marketing mix are described. Because you are trying to appeal to computer users, use a computer to create and print your flyer if possible.

Name ______________________________ Date __________ Class ____________________

Lesson 12.1 Business-To-Business Exchanges

LESSON QUIZ

Directions For each of the following statements, if the statement is true, write a T on the answer line; if the statement is false, write an F on the answer line.

_____ 1. The various types of products and services that businesses buy and sell can be organized within the business product classification system.

_____ 2. A producer or manufacturer must purchase everything it needs to develop the products it sells.

_____ 3. Some business purchase products for direct resale to consumers.

_____ 4. While there are differences between business consumers and final consumers, the marketing process used for each group is basically the same.

_____ 5. There are more producers in the United States than the total number of resellers and service businesses combined.

_____ 6. The total purchases made by the U.S. government make it the largest single customer in the world.

_____ 7. The U.S. military operates like wholesalers and retailers when it purchases products for distribution and resale to military personnel and their families.

_____ 8. The number of business customers for specific products is usually smaller than the number of final consumers who will purchase a product.

Directions For each of the following items, decide which choice best completes the statement. Write the letter that identifies your choice on the answer line.

_____ 9. To market products to businesses, a supplier must
A. identify the target market
B. determine the characteristics and needs of the target market
C. develop a marketing mix
D. all of the above

_____10. Businesses that purchase products for resale are
A. producers
B. wholesale and retail businesses
C. producers and retailers
D. wholesalers and producers

_____11. Which of the following is not a characteristic of business markets?
A. a business's demand is derived from the demand of its customers
B. business customers generally purchase in larger quantities than final consumers
C. businesses that resell similar products usually have quite different purchase needs
D. businesses that produce products for sale to final consumers often have little contact with the customer

Activity 1 • Classify Business Purchasers and Purchases

Directions Use a business directory, the Internet, or your own experience to identify a business in your community that fits each of the categories of business purchasers. Then for each business, identify one product they might purchase that fits each of the business purchase classifications.

Category	Business	Purchase Classification	Product Purchased by the Business
Producer		Capital goods	
		Operating equipment	
		Raw materials	
		Component parts	
		Services	
Reseller—Wholesaler		Capital goods	
		Operating equipment	
		Raw materials	
		Component parts	
		Services	
Reseller—Retailer		Capital goods	
		Operating equipment	
		Raw materials	
		Component parts	
		Services	
Service		Capital goods	
		Operating equipment	
		Raw materials	
		Component parts	
		Services	
Government Agency		Capital goods	
		Operating equipment	
		Raw materials	
		Component parts	
		Services	
Nonprofit Organization		Capital goods	
		Operating equipment	
		Raw materials	
		Component parts	
		Services	

Name ______________________ Date __________ Class ______________

Lesson 12.2 Make Business Purchase Decisions

LESSON QUIZ

Directions For each of the following statements, if the statement is true, write a T on the answer line; if the statement is false, write an F on the answer line.

_____ 1. A business will purchase the product or service that meets its needs at a reasonable price. Cost-effective purchases contribute to profits.

_____ 2. Rather than buying a needed product or service, a business may decide to make the item with its own resources.

_____ 3. Most businesses seldom purchase from the same supplier repeatedly.

_____ 4. The reorder point is the level of inventory needed to meet the usage needs of the business until the product can be resupplied.

_____ 5. A purchasing process may become so routine that it is handled by a computer.

_____ 6. When many companies offer the same product for sale, repeat purchasing becomes very competitive.

_____ 7. The easiest purchasing decision for a company is when it buys a product or service for the first time.

_____ 8. Reciprocal trading is a form of bartering in which the products or services of one company are used as payment for the products or services of another company.

Directions For each of the following items, decide which choice best completes the statement. Write the letter that identifies your choice on the answer line.

_____ 9. The product or service a business purchases will be the one that
- A. has the highest quality
- B. meets the need at a reasonable price
- C. has the lowest price
- D. can be resold to customers

_____10. A business making a new purchase must
- A. determine what needs it must meet with the purchase
- B. decide upon the types of products that can meet its needs
- C. identify the companies that offer the needed products
- D. all of the above

_____11. Which of the following applies to international purchasing?
- A. Businesses should purchase from other businesses in their home country even when participating in international trade.
- B. It is usually very easy to negotiate prices between two different countries.
- C. Businesses should use a bank that has established relationships with financial institutions in other countries.
- D. The time needed for transporting products to other countries is always longer than domestic shipments.

Activity 1 • Diagram a Buying Decision

Directions Assume you are a buyer for a large manufacturer. Develop a flow chart integrating the three types of buying decisions and the steps involved in making business purchases as described in your textbook. A flow chart is a pictorial description of information flowing along a chain of decisions. List each decision in the sequence in which it is made and the possible results. One type of decision is shown as an example.

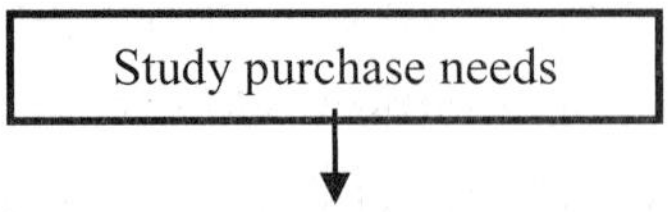

Name ______________________________ Date __________ Class ____________________

Lesson 12.3 Business Purchasing Procedures

LESSON QUIZ

Directions For each of the following statements, if the statement is true, write a T on the answer line; if the statement is false, write an F on the answer line.

_____ 1. The purchasing process a business follows is usually simpler and more streamlined than the purchasing process followed by an individual consumer.

_____ 2. The needs of different parts of a business may conflict with each other.

_____ 3. The most restrictive type of negotiation is known as bidding.

_____ 4. The final step in the purchasing decision by business customers is different from that for final consumers.

_____ 5. Companies should always select the vendor that offers the highest-quality product.

_____ 6. When several people are involved in the purchase decision in a business, it may involve conflict and politics.

_____ 7. A perpetual inventory system determines the amount of product on hand by visually inspecting and counting the items.

_____ 8. A buyer completes a packing list which states the quantity and prices of all the products included in the shipment.

Directions For each of the following items, decide which choice best completes the statement. Write the letter that identifies your choice on the answer line.

_____ 9. An objective rating system buyers use to compare potential suppliers on important purchasing criteria is a
A. supplier rating
B. vendor analysis
C. total quality management system
D. buyer's need scale

_____10. A company that develops a relationship with its suppliers which enables it to keep inventory levels low and to resupply inventory when it is needed is using
A. just-in-time supply
B. total quality management
C. new product purchasing
D. supply chain planning

_____11. Two types of inventory systems used in businesses are
A. input and output
B. annual and continuous
C. physical and perpetual
D. wholesale and retail

Activity 1 • Functional Relationships

Directions Purchasing is one of the nine marketing functions that is essential for the profitable operation of a business. Using the list provided, indicate how purchasing benefits or relates to each of the remaining functions. The first answer is provided.

Marketing Function	Benefit or Relationship to Purchasing
Market Planning	*As new markets and marketing mixes are identified, businesses determine their purchasing needs to develop and market the new products and services.*
Product and Service Management	
Pricing	
Promotion	
Selling	
Distribution	
Marketing-Information Management	
Financing	
Risk Management	

Name ____ Date ____________ Class__________________________

Lesson 12.4 Retail Purchasing

LESSON QUIZ

Directions For each of the following statements, if the statement is true, write a T on the answer line; if the statement is false, write an F on the answer line.

_____ 1. Most retailers collect customer and product information each time a sale is made.

_____ 2. Computer technology helps retailers track the sales of current products to determine which products sell rapidly and which do not.

_____ 3. Most stores develop merchandise plans for several years at a time.

_____ 4. A model stock list identifies the minimum amount of important products the store needs to have available to meet the needs of its target market.

_____ 5. Retailers purchase items from both manufacturers and wholesalers.

_____ 6. Because there are so many large retailers, vendors no longer have salespeople make personal visits to retail buyers.

_____ 7. Because most retail businesses have very low profit margins, any significant loss during the receiving process can affect the business's ability to make a profit.

Directions For each of the following items, decide which choice best completes the statement. Write the letter that identifies your choice on the answer line.

_____ 8. For which types of retail purchasing are merchandise catalogs and vendor websites particularly useful?
A. standardized products sold primarily on the basis of price and availability
B. purchases by small businesses who cannot afford to attend trade shows and purchase in small quantities
C. routine purchases of regular customers
D. all of the above

_____ 9. A retailer's basic stock list
A. is reordered infrequently
B. identifies the complete assortment of products a store would like to offer its customers
C. will not change much over time
D. is more extensive than the model stock list

_____10. Which of the following is not true about retail purchasing decisions?
A. For fast-selling or perishable products, the most important factor for a vendor is offering a low price.
B. Retailers may not be certain of the total inventory that can be sold for fashions or seasonal products and so will want a vendor that can quickly provide additional quantities.
C. The timing of orders to be sure adequate inventory is available when needed is a difficult decision.
D. All are true.

Activity 1 • Reorder Tote Bags

Directions Sue owns an arts and crafts store. She needs to reorder tote bags for the fall season. The vendor prices are shown in the following table.

	Case (4 dozen)	Dozen	Unit
Canvas tote:			
Natural	$ 98.40	$25.08	$2.15
Black, green, navy, red	110.40	28.20	2.41
Nylon fanny pack	122.88	31.44	2.69
Jumbo tote	164.64	42.24	3.60
Zipper tote	159.85	40.92	3.49
Deluxe tote (natural)	153.12	39.25	3.35

Last year, Sue carried only the canvas tote and the deluxe tote. She sold 10 dozen natural canvas totes and 8 3/4 dozen natural deluxe totes. Although she does not do any formal market research, Sue has the following information:

- Sales are up 5 percent from last year.
- This year she has scheduled five craft classes with 12 students per class. Each student will have to purchase a natural canvas tote.

Answer the following questions:

1. How many natural canvas totes does Sue need to order to cover the expected increase in business and the scheduled classes? What is the cost of this order?

   ____

2. How many natural deluxe totes does she need to order to cover her anticipated sales? What is the cost of this order?

   ____

3. What is the total cost for purchasing the natural canvas totes and natural deluxe totes?

   ____

4. In addition to the natural totes, Sue also placed the following order. What is its total cost?

Item	Cost
2 doz. nylon fanny packs	
2 doz. zipper totes	
1 doz. navy canvas totes	
1 doz. black canvas totes	
4 doz. red canvas totes	
4 doz. green canvas totes	
2 doz. jumbo totes	
Total cost	

Name ______________________________ Date __________ Class ________________

Lesson 13.1 Marketing Through Distribution

LESSON QUIZ

Directions For each of the following statements, if the statement is true, write a T on the answer line; if the statement is false, write an F on the answer line.

_____ 1. Distribution is the most challenging and complex part of marketing.

_____ 2. For most products, distribution accounts for about 10 percent of total marketing costs.

_____ 3. Distribution has only become an important part of marketing in the past 50 years.

_____ 4. Because a free enterprise economy is based on the matching of production and consumption, distribution is essential to the effectiveness of free enterprise.

_____ 5. Distribution as a part of the marketing mix involves the locations and methods used to make the product available to customers.

_____ 6. The success of a product or a business is usually influenced by many other businesses.

_____ 7. A producer only has to be concerned about where the product is produced, not where it will be sold or used.

Directions For each of the following items, decide which choice best completes the statement. Write the letter that identifies your choice on the answer line.

_____ 8. The oldest and most basic part of marketing is
A. distribution
B. production
C. advertising
D. placing an order

_____ 9. The amount of satisfaction a consumer receives from the consumption of a particular product or service is
A. product satisfaction
B. consumption satisfaction
C. economic utility
D. based solely on distribution

_____10. Businesses that apply the marketing concept will fail if each company involved in distribution
A. is not involved in developing the product
B. does not follow the marketing plan
C. does not use the lowest-cost methods available
D. all of the above

_____11. All of the following are distribution decisions except
A. When will each activity occur?
B. What characteristics of the product or service will affect distribution?
C. Who is responsible for planning and managing the distribution process?
D. What aspects of the distribution process will be described in promotional efforts?

Activity 1 • More than Distribution

Directions Review articles and stories in business magazines, newspapers, and on the Internet about businesses that are involved in product distribution. Find information about how the distribution activities are related to or affected by each of the other marketing functions. Write a brief description of each example in the space provided.

Selling: ____________________

Promotion: ____________________

Risk Management: ____________________

Pricing: ____________________

Marketing-Information Management: ____________________

Product and Service management: ____________________

Financing: ____________________

Market Planning: ____________________

Activity 2 • Move Products Around the World

Directions Identify three manufacturers from your area that have important markets for their products in several other countries. Using information obtained directly from the companies or the Internet, determine where the products are distributed and sold.

Manufacturer: ____________________ Product: ____________________

Sold in:

Country 1: ____________________

Country 2: ____________________

Country 3: ____________________

Country 4: ____________________

Manufacturer: ____________________ Product: ____________________

Sold in:

Country 1: ____________________

Country 2: ____________________

Country 3: ____________________

Country 4: ____________________

Manufacturer: ____________________ Product: ____________________

Sold in:

Country 1: ____________________

Country 2: ____________________

Country 3: ____________________

Country 4: ____________________

Name ______________________________ Date __________ Class ________________

Lesson 13.2 Distribution Channels

LESSON QUIZ

Directions For each of the following statements, if the statement is true, write a T on the answer line; if the statement is false, write an F on the answer line.

_____ 1. Some products and services do not require a channel of distribution.

_____ 2. What producers develop and what customers need often differ.

_____ 3. Most businesses sell their products to a limited number of customers who purchase the quantity they need for personal consumption.

_____ 4. A channel of distribution accumulates products from a number of manufacturers and makes them available in one location to give consumers adequate choice and variety.

_____ 5. A channel of distribution is necessary to move the product from the place where it is produced to the place where it will be consumed.

_____ 6. An indirect channel of distribution is most often selected when consumers are located in a small geographic area.

_____ 7. Channel management is most effective when members work to meet their own goals.

Directions For each of the following items, decide which choice best completes the statement. Write the letter that identifies your choice on the answer line.

_____ 8. When products and services are exchanged, they move through a

A. product pipeline
B. single distributor
C. channel of distribution
D. business exchange network

_____ 9. In the exchange between producer and consumer,

A. only the producer is responsible for completing all of the marketing functions
B. only the consumer is responsible for completing all of the marketing functions
C. channel members complete only distribution activities
D. each channel member may be responsible for completing some of the marketing functions in addition to distribution

_____10. Managing a channel of distribution is the responsibility of the

A. consumers
B. channel captain
C. reseller
D. manufacturer or producer

_____11. The technology that allows for the efficient exchange of information among departments in a company is known as

A. CRM
B. SCM
C. EDI
D. none of the above

Activity 1 • Local Grocery Store, International Products

Directions Your local grocery store offers perishable foods that are produced around the world. Getting those products from the suppliers to their customers in the best possible condition is a challenge of the international channel of distribution. Visit a local grocery store. Identify two items in each product category listed below sold in the store. Check labels to identify the producer or distributor and location of production. Make sure at least one product in each category is produced outside the United States. Identify any special handling the product needs during distribution. Evaluate the freshness, appearance, and quality of the product.

Fresh Fruit

Product: ______________________ Producer: ______________________

Special Handling: ______________________ Location: ______________________

Product Evaluation: ____

Product: ______________________ Producer: ______________________

Special Handling: ______________________ Location: ______________________

Product Evaluation: ____

Baked Goods

Product: ______________________ Producer: ______________________

Special Handling: ______________________ Location: ______________________

Product Evaluation: ____

Product: ______________________ Producer: ______________________

Special Handling: ______________________ Location: ______________________

Product Evaluation: ____

Meat

Product: ______________________ Producer: ______________________

Special Handling: ______________________ Location: ______________________

Product Evaluation: ____

Product: ______________________ Producer: ______________________

Special Handling: ______________________ Location: ______________________

Product Evaluation: ____

Frozen Foods

Product: ______________________ Producer: ______________________

Special Handling: ______________________ Location: ______________________

Product Evaluation: ____

Product: ______________________ Producer: ______________________

Special Handling: ______________________ Location: ______________________

Product Evaluation: ____

Name ______________________________ Date __________ Class ______________

Lesson 13.3 The Role of Wholesaling

LESSON QUIZ

Directions For each of the following statements, if the statement is true, write a T on the answer line; if the statement is false, write an F on the answer line.

_____ 1. Marketing functions can be shifted or shared, but they cannot be eliminated in a channel of distribution.

_____ 2. Wholesalers work as frequently with final consumers as they do with manufacturers and retailers.

_____ 3. The advantage of wholesalers is that they can always complete distribution activities at a lower cost than either manufacturers or retailers.

_____ 4. Wholesalers accumulate the products of many manufacturers, develop appropriate assortments for their customers, and distribute the products to them.

_____ 5. Small and medium-sized businesses use wholesalers because they need effective purchasing and distribution methods to compete with large businesses.

_____ 6. Export and import firms are examples of international wholesalers.

_____ 7. Wholesalers can use technology to provide marketing information management services to their customers.

Directions For each of the following items, decide which choice best completes the statement. Write the letter that identifies your choice on the answer line.

_____ 8. A wholesaler becomes part of a channel of distribution when
- A. there are too many retailers for a manufacturer to serve efficiently
- B. a retailer works with a large number of producers
- C. the wholesaler is able to complete a large number of marketing tasks that manufacturers or retailers do not want to perform
- D. all of the above

_____ 9. A wholesale member club targets
- A. small businesses
- B. employees of large businesses and organizations
- C. individual consumers
- D. all of the above

_____10. Wholesale businesses owned by producers or retailers to provide distribution services to members are known as
- A. wholesale cooperatives
- B. full-service wholesalers
- C. limited-service wholesalers
- D. brokers

Activity 1 • Moving Potato Chips

Directions Potato chips are sold by retailers to both final consumers for consumption and business consumers for resale. Connect the appropriate channel members so that each consumer gets potato chips through a logical channel. Be prepared to explain your decisions.

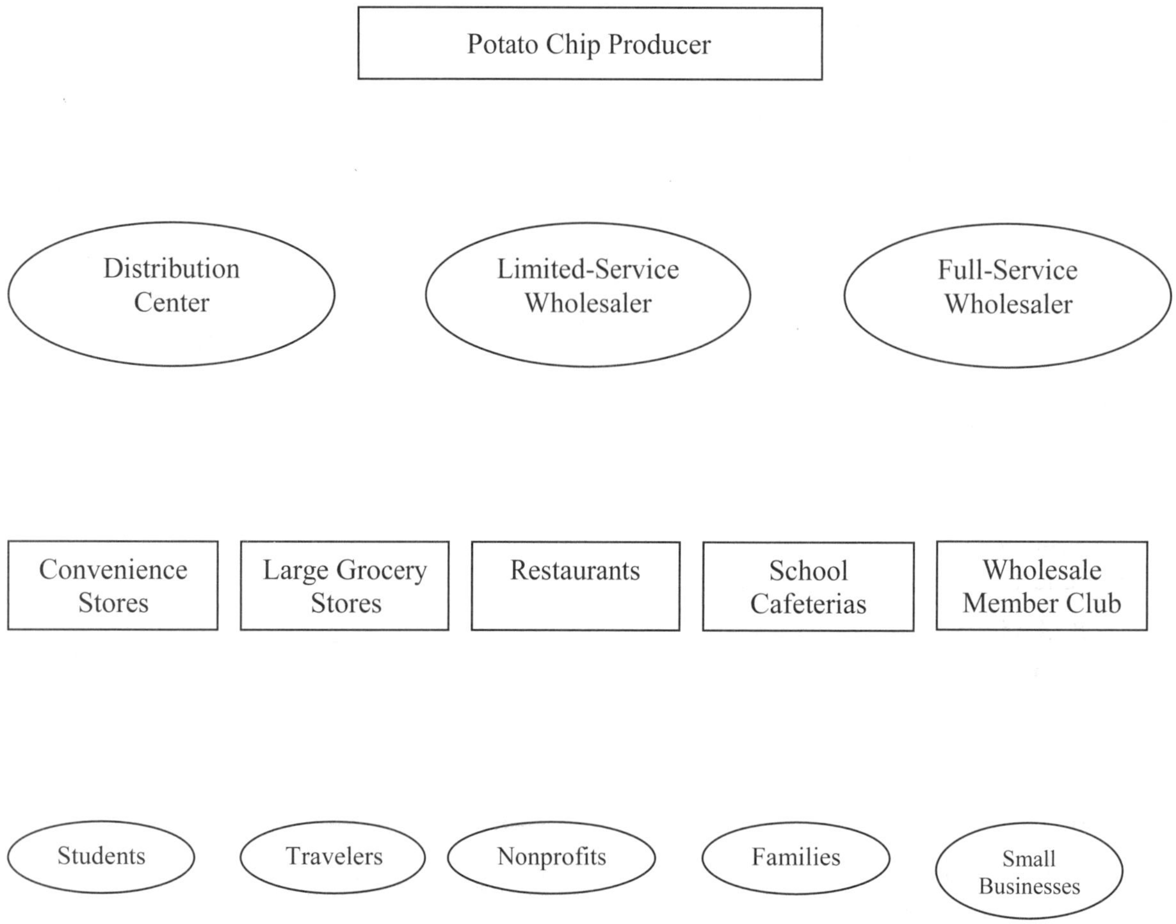

Activity 2 • Membership Has Benefits

Directions Contact a nearby wholesale club or visit the Internet site for Sam's Club, BJ's Wholesale Club, or Costco Wholesale. Gather information and answer the following questions.

Membership requirements: ______________________________

____

Membership levels: ______________________________

____

Cost of membership: ______________________________

____

Membership benefits: ______________________________

____

Name ____ Date ____________ Class_________________________

Lesson 13.4 The Role of Retailing

LESSON QUIZ

Directions For each of the following statements, if the statement is true, write a T on the answer line; if the statement is false, write an F on the answer line.

_____ 1. Primary customers of retailers are individuals purchasing to meet their own needs.

_____ 2. Retailers purchase products only from wholesalers.

_____ 3. Retailers store large amounts of inventory of products so customers will have a variety of product choices and ready availability if they decide to purchase.

_____ 4. All retailers offer a wide variety of choices from many product categories.

_____ 5. Businesses that offer services as their primary business are not considered to be retailers.

_____ 6. Non-store retailing involves selling directly to the consumer at home rather than requiring the consumer to travel to a store.

_____ 7. Because retailers must appeal to all types of consumers, they try to reduce the amount of technology used in the business.

Directions For each of the following items, decide which choice best completes the statement. Write the letter that identifies your choice on the answer line.

_____ 8. An important way of categorizing retailers is by the
A. characteristics of their customers
B. types of products offered
C. area of a town or city where they are located
D. name of the store

_____ 9. The owner of a franchise that develops a basic business plan and operating procedures for the business is the
A. franchiser
B. franchisee
C. financer
D. channel captain

_____10. The elements of the shopping environment that are appealing to customers, attract them to a store, and encourage them to buy are known as
A. the store layout
B. the shopping experience
C. atmospherics
D. a competitive advantage

_____11. Retailers offering products from one merchandise category or closely related items are
A. mixed merchandise retailers
B. limited-line retailers
C. service retailers
D. non-store retailers

Activity 1 • Specialty Retailers

Directions Select a nearby specialty retailer you can visit. Answer the following questions.

Retailer: ______________________________

Product category(ies) and variety: ______________________________

____

____

Target market description: ______________________________

____

____

How does the retailer try to make its marketing mix unique and appealing to the target market?

____

____

____

Activity 2 • Retail Location and Atmospherics

Directions Location and atmospherics are important to all retailers that expect customers to visit the retail store. Select a nearby retailer and evaluate the following factors related to location and atmospherics that contribute to a positive shopping experience.

Retailer: ______________ Location: ______________

Type of retailer: ______________ Target market: ______________

Nearby retailers or other businesses: ______________________________

Appearance of the building: ______________________________

Signage: ______________________________

Amount and quality of parking: ______________________________

Amount of vehicle, public transportation, and foot traffic: ______________________________

Positive and negative traffic pattern factors (traffic lights, medians, one-way streets, etc.): ______

____

Accessibility from major roads: ______________________________

Overall impression of retailer atmospherics: ______________________________

____

Name ____ Date ____________ Class__________________________

Lesson 13.5 Physical Distribution

LESSON QUIZ

Directions For each of the following statements, if the statement is true, write a T on the answer line; if the statement is false, write an F on the answer line.

_____ 1. Another name for physical distribution is logistics.

_____ 2. Physical distribution includes financing the product as it moves through the channel of distribution.

_____ 3. Products are often grouped into large units for transportation and then divided into smaller units for display, sale, storage, or use.

_____ 4. Railroads are particularly useful for carrying a large quantity of small products that need to be delivered quickly.

_____ 5. Air transportation is the best choice for delivering products long distances rapidly.

_____ 6. Pipelines are expensive to construct and can be difficult to maintain.

_____ 7. Most products are delivered from the manufacturer to the final customer using a single transportation method.

_____ 8. An inventory control system should identify how much of each product is being sold and how rapidly.

Directions For each of the following items, decide which choice best completes the statement. Write the letter that identifies your choice on the answer line.

_____ 9. Factors involved in selecting a transportation method for products include the
A. location where the product is to be delivered
B. type of product to be shipped
C. speed of delivery
D. all of the above

_____10. The most flexible major transportation method is
A. railroads
B. trucks
C. ships and boats
D. air

_____11. A facility used to accumulate products from several sources and then regroup, repackage, and send them as quickly as possible to the locations where they will be used is a
A. distribution center
B. central exchange facility
C. warehouse
D. factory outlet

Activity 1 • Special Requirements in Distribution

Directions Think about the process of producing, distributing, and selling three different types of products: fresh flowers, backpacks, and tropical birds. Each provides a different distribution challenge. Answer the following questions for each product. Use additional sheets of paper if necessary.

1. Where will the product be produced?
2. Where will the product be used?
3. Where will the product be exchanged?
4. What characteristics of the product will affect distribution?
5. What type of special handling is needed?
6. What type of risks will the distributor face?

Fresh flowers:____

____

____

Backpacks:____

____

____

Tropical birds:____

____

____

Activity 2 • Trans-Alaska Pipeline

Directions The Trans-Alaska pipeline provides 17 percent of America's domestic crude oil production. Use the library or Internet to answer the following questions.

When was the pipeline constructed?______________________________

When did the first oil move through the pipeline?______________________________

How long is the pipeline?______________________________

How much of the pipeline is above ground?__________ Below ground? __________

What is the diameter of the pipe?______________________________

Where does the pipeline start and end? ______________________________

How much oil has moved through the pipeline? ______________________________

How much did it cost to build the pipeline?______________________________

Who owns the pipeline?______________________________

____

____

Name ______________________ Date __________ Class ______________

Lesson 14.1 The Economics of Price Decisions

LESSON QUIZ

Directions For each of the following statements, if the statement is true, write a T on the answer line; if the statement is false, write an F on the answer line.

_____ 1. The lowest price is always the best price for every customer.

_____ 2. Price is an important tool for marketers because it can be changed more quickly than other marketing decisions.

_____ 3. Price allocates available resources among people.

_____ 4. If sales increase, profits will increase as well.

_____ 5. If you lower the price of your product, you will sell a larger quantity of the product and always increase profit margin.

_____ 6. In the United States, it is illegal for two competing companies to agree on the amount they will charge for products or services.

_____ 7. It is illegal for a business to lure a customer into a store by offering a low price and then telling the customer that the low-priced product is unavailable.

Directions For each of the following items, decide which choice best completes the statement. Write the letter that identifies your choice on the answer line.

_____ 8. When companies advertise a low price but then tell customers the product is unavailable or inferior, this practice is known as
A. price fixing
B. unit pricing
C. price discrimination
D. bait and switch

_____ 9. The relationship between changes in a product's price and the demand for that product is known as
A. equilibrium price
B. elasticity of demand
C. economic utility
D. price/demand ratio

_____10. In a private enterprise economy, governments
A. encourage activities that benefit society
B. determine product prices
C. prevent companies from growing
D. all of the above

Activity 1 • Business Information

Directions Pricing strategies are used every day by businesses to attract attention and gain customers. Look at a local newspaper and clip five advertisements that use price as part of the promotional strategy. Mount each advertisement on a separate sheet of paper and provide the following information for each ad:

1. Name of the business
2. Item being advertised
3. Target market for this item
4. Type of competition for this item
5. Type of pricing techniques used

Directions Locate five advertisements that use non-pricing strategies. Clip and mount these ads on separate sheets of paper and provide the following information:

1. Name of the business
2. Item being advertised
3. Target market for this item
4. Type of competition for this item
5. Unique quality of the item that is being advertised

Activity 2 • It's the Law

Directions Using the library or Internet, research two laws that relate to pricing of products by businesses. Answer the following questions.

Name of the law: ______________________________

Date the law was enacted: ______________________________

Purpose of the law: ______________________________

Is the law still in existence? ______________________________

How does the law help businesses? ______________________________

____

____

How does the law help consumers? ______________________________

____

____

Name of the law: ______________________________

Date the law was enacted: ______________________________

Purpose of the law: ______________________________

Is the law still in existence? ______________________________

How does the law help businesses? ______________________________

____

____

How does the law help consumers? ______________________________

____

____

Name ________________________________ Date __________ Class ________________

Lesson 14.2 Develop Pricing Procedures

LESSON QUIZ

Directions For each of the following statements, if the statement is true, write a T on the answer line; if the statement is false, write an F on the answer line.

_____ 1. Companies that want to maximize profits study consumer demand to determine what customers in the target market are willing to pay for their products.

_____ 2. Sales-based pricing objectives set prices to achieve the highest possible sales volume.

_____ 3. A company that does not post prices with its product is trying to appeal to cost-conscious customers.

_____ 4. The difference between the product cost and the selling price is known as an operating expense.

_____ 5. High markups do not always mean that a business will make a larger profit on overall sales.

_____ 6. A company can determine the minimum price by performing a breakeven analysis.

_____ 7. Fixed costs are determined by the quantity of the product that is produced or sold.

Directions For each of the following items, decide which choice best completes the statement. Write the letter that identifies your choice on the answer line.

_____ 8. At the breakeven point, a company

A. maximizes profits
B. needs to increase its price
C. matches total costs and total revenues
D. suffers the greatest losses

_____ 9. Markdowns

A. are usually viewed as a business mistake because the product did not sell well at the planned price
B. can be expressed as a specific dollar amount or as a percentage of the original selling price
C. are used when products are not selling well
D. all are correct

_____10. ____________ is/are an amount added to the cost of a product to determine the selling price.

A. Markup
B. Gross margin
C. Operating costs
D. Net profit

Activity 1 • Calculate Costs

Directions Use the following information to answer the questions below.

Sierra has opened a small business designing T-shirts. The current selling price is $28 per shirt.

Costs of Goods Sold for Each Shirt	
Shirts	$8
Related materials	4
Ironing and sewing	2
Monthly Fixed Costs	
Rent	$100
Utilities	30
Transportation	25
Postage	30
Miscellaneous	20
Sales Last Year	
Month	**Units Sold**
January	15
February	20
March	25
April	50
May	75
June	15
July	18
August	5
September	20
October	250
November	225
December	15

What is Sierra's total revenue?

____

What is the total cost of goods sold?

____

What is the gross margin?

____

What are the total fixed costs for the year?

____

What is Sierra's net profit?

____

What is the breakeven point?

____

What is the markup as a percentage of the selling price?

____

What is the markup as a percentage of cost?

____

Name ______________________________ Date __________ Class ____________________

Lesson 14.3 Pricing Based on Market Conditions

LESSON QUIZ

Directions For each of the following statements, if the statement is true, write a T on the answer line; if the statement is false, write an F on the answer line.

_____ 1. The type of competition a product faces changes throughout the stages of its life cycle.

_____ 2. During the introductory stage, only one brand of a new product is available allowing the business a great deal of control over the price.

_____ 3. A penetration price usually results in higher profits for the company but encourages other companies to enter the market.

_____ 4. In later stages of the life cycle, competition decreases with less emphasis on price competition.

_____ 5. Intensive price competition is a characteristic of both staple convenience goods and price-based shopping goods.

_____ 6. "FOB factory" means the manufacturer will pay all transportation costs from the point where the product is manufactured to the location of the customer.

_____ 7. With zone pricing, different product or transportation costs are set for specific areas of the seller's market.

_____ 8. Coupons and rebates are examples of discounts and allowances used by businesses.

Directions For each of the following items, decide which choice best completes the statement. Write the letter that identifies your choice on the answer line.

_____ 9. Distinct categories of prices based on differences in product quality and features are
- A. skimming prices
- B. price lines
- C. geographic prices
- D. discounts and allowances

_____10. A business can change the perception of the value of a product by
- A. making additions to the purchase
- B. offering a special deal such as "buy one, get one free"
- C. offering an incentive for making a purchase
- D. all are correct

_____11. Credit offered by one business to another is
- A. retail credit
- B. trade credit
- C. flexible pricing
- D. illegal

Activity 1 • Change Sales and Prices

Directions Create a flow chart that identifies the stages in a product's life cycle. Include a description of what to expect from sales and prices in each stage.

Activity 2 • Manage Price Strategies

Directions The product life cycle helps marketers determine how to price their products based on competition and the uniqueness of the products. Your company has developed a unique new sunscreen product. It is guaranteed to last all day. It is waterproof, odorless, colorless, and will not wipe off or stain clothing. The following chart describes four different market scenarios. For each scenario, complete the chart by determining what stage of the life cycle the sunscreen is in and what type of pricing strategy would be appropriate.

Market Description	Life-Cycle Stage	Pricing Strategy
Customers love your product and buy it. Competitors rush to introduce similar products.		
Your company has the only product of its type in the market, and it is positioned as a "premium" product.		
A new "organic" product is introduced that is promoted as better than sunscreen. Customers begin to try it and your sales take a hit.		
With many brands available, you find competitors offering coupons and increasing their distribution.		

Name ______________________________ Date ____________ Class ______________________

Lesson 15.1 Promotion as a Form of Communication

LESSON QUIZ

Directions For each of the following statements, if the statement is true, write a T on the answer line; if the statement is false, write an F on the answer line.

_____ 1. Advertising is any form of communication that a company uses to inform, persuade, or remind consumers about its products or services.

_____ 2. In marketing, the sender of a message is typically the advertising agency.

_____ 3. Several messages can be sent at the same time in the promotional process.

_____ 4. Encoding is putting a message into language or symbols familiar to the receiver.

_____ 5. The message channel is how the message will be distributed.

_____ 6. Feedback is not necessary in most promotions because they are planned by communications experts.

_____ 7. Providing information to consumers is important for complex products and services.

_____ 8. Interpersonal communication attempts to reach large numbers of people with one message.

Directions For each of the following items, decide which choice best completes the statement. Write the letter that identifies your choice on the answer line.

_____ 9. Mass communication is
A. the opposite of interpersonal communication
B. a one-way flow of information
C. can be much more cost-efficient than personal selling
D. all of the above

_____10. The receiver's reaction or response to the source's message is
A. noise
B. always a purchase
C. feedback
D. agreement

_____11. When a business needs to make a case for why customers should buy its product, the promotional goal should be to
A. inform
B. persuade
C. remind
D. encourage

_____12. *Monday Night Football* is an example of a promotional
A. media
B. vehicle
C. receiver
D. sender

Activity 1 • Inform, Persuade, and Remind

Directions The purpose of promotion is to inform, persuade, and remind the consumer of products and services. As products move through the product life cycle, marketers use various promotional tools to convey messages to their target audiences. Choose a product that is familiar to most consumers and purchased regularly. In the spaces below, sketch an informational billboard, a persuasive billboard, and a reminder billboard.

Informational Billboard

Persuasive Billboard

Reminder Billboard

Name ______________________________ Date __________ Class ______________________

Lesson 15.2 Types of Promotion

LESSON QUIZ

Directions For each of the following statements, if the statement is true, write a T on the answer line; if the statement is false, write an F on the answer line.

_____ 1. Direct mail is a form of advertising.

_____ 2. Billboards are just one form of outdoor advertising.

_____ 3. The fastest-growing and most dynamic form of advertising today is TV advertising.

_____ 4. Publicity is any nonpaid mention of a product, service, company, or cause.

_____ 5. The major disadvantage of publicity is that it is hard to control.

_____ 6. The types of products for which personal selling is appropriate are usually complicated and relatively expensive products with many features.

_____ 7. A disadvantage of personal selling is the difficulty of responding to individual customer needs.

_____ 8. Coupons, rebates, contests, and product samples are all examples of sales promotion.

Directions For each of the following items, decide which choice best completes the statement. Write the letter that identifies your choice on the answer line.

_____ 9. Which of the following is an example of broadcast media?

A. television
B. radio
C. magazine
D. both a and b

_____10. Stickers on bananas, messages chalked onto sidewalks, hot-air balloons, stunts or "guerilla" advertising, and messages on bathroom stall doors are examples of

A. publicity
B. ambient advertising
C. outdoor advertising
D. sales promotion

_____11. A disadvantage of __________________ is that it can encourage customers to buy a product for reasons other than a true preference for the brand.

A. advertising
B. personal selling
C. publicity
D. sales promotion

_____12. An advantage of __________________ is that a third-party source is often viewed by consumers to be more trustworthy than a commercial.

A. advertising
B. personal selling
C. publicity
D. sales promotion

Activity 1 • Publicity

Directions Stories about major area businesses are often published in local newspapers. Review several recent issues of the newspaper for your community. Locate a story about a business operating in your community. Based on the article, answer the following questions.

1. What is the name of the business? ______________________________

2. What is the type of business? What products and services does it sell? ______________________________

3. What information did you learn about the business? ______________________________

4. What was the primary reason for the article? ______________________________

5. Will this article create goodwill among consumers? Why or why not? ______________________________

6. Does it appear the business was actively involved in developing the article? Explain.______________________________

Activity 2 • Sales Promotions

Directions Find an example of a current attention-getting sales promotion product or activity. Use it to answer the following questions.

1. What is the name of the business sponsoring the promotion? ______________________________

2. What is the good or service produced by the company? ______________________________

3. Who is the target market for the good or service? ______________________________

4. What makes the sales promotion attention-getting and unique?______________________________

5. What do you believe is the purpose of the sales promotion? Do you think it achieves that purpose? Explain.______________________________

Name ______________________________ Date __________ Class ____________________

Lesson 15.3 The Promotional Plan

LESSON QUIZ

Directions For each of the following statements, if the statement is true, write a T on the answer line; if the statement is false, write an F on the answer line.

_____ 1. The promotional mix includes the product, distribution, price, and promotion.

_____ 2. A company's product promotions should be consistent with its philosophy.

_____ 3. No matter which type of promotion is selected, it serves the same purpose in the promotional mix.

_____ 4. The blueprint for how the elements of the promotional mix will work together is called the marketing plan.

_____ 5. Before beginning promotional planning, the promotional budget should be established.

_____ 6. Marketers should evaluate their promotional plans during and after promotions.

_____ 7. The results of promotions should be compared to the promotional objectives to determine if they were accomplished.

Directions For each of the following items, decide which choice best completes the statement. Write the letter that identifies your choice on the answer line.

_____ 8. __________________ is an excellent tool for informing customers and delivering large quantities of information.
- A. Advertising
- B. Personal selling
- C. Publicity
- D. Sales promotion

_____ 9. The promotional mix is the combination of all of the following elements except
- A. advertising
- B. public relations
- C. personal selling
- D. all of the above are elements of the promotional mix

_____10. Which of the following activities occurs after the promotional mix is developed?
- A. select the target market
- B. establish promotional objectives
- C. develop an activity schedule
- D. all of the above

_____11. Which of the following activities involves attempts to gain an understanding of the market?
- A. research and analyze the market
- B. select the target market
- C. identify promotional objectives
- D. set the promotional budget

Activity 1 • Coupon Popularity

Directions The use of coupons is a major sales promotion tool for many manufacturers and retailers. In an effort to determine the effectiveness of coupons, a consumer products manufacturing association completed a consumer opinion study of attitudes toward the use of coupons by businesses. The survey was repeated five years later to determine if attitudes had changed. Responses for both studies are shown in the table.

Attitudes Toward Coupons	Original Study		Repeated Study		Change in Attitude (+/-)
Favorable	350		417		
Somewhat Favorable	373		313		
Somewhat Unfavorable	23		16		
Very unfavorable	48		26		

1. Calculate the percentage of total responses for each category for each study, rounding off to the nearest whole number.
2. Calculate the percentage increase or decrease for each category.
3. What conclusions can you draw from the results? ____________________
4. Why do you believe the figures changed? ____________________
5. Do you believe consumer attitudes about coupons have changed since the study was last conducted? Explain. ____________________

Activity 2 • Effective Publicity

Directions Each year your school participates in developing a special section of the local newspaper titled "Up with Education." This section updates the community on education in general and provides features on school programs and activities. Your teacher has asked you to write an article on Marketing Education and its unique contributions to the school and community. Your goal is to provide positive publicity for the program. Your article should be between 300 to 500 words.

Name ____ Date ____________ Class__________________________

Lesson 16.1 What Is Advertising?

LESSON QUIZ

Directions For each of the following statements, if the statement is true, write a T on the answer line; if the statement is false, write an F on the answer line.

_____ 1. In the United States, total expenditures for advertising are just under $100 billion a year.

_____ 2. Brand advertising is advertising that aims to build an image.

_____ 3. Almost all companies do their own advertising rather than hire an advertising agency.

_____ 4. An account executive is the key liaison between the client and the agency.

_____ 5. The goal of a media plan is to give the business the best coverage of its target market for the least amount of money.

_____ 6. In an advertising agency, the art director guides the creative process and ensures the creative team's work conveys the right message and is in line with the client's needs.

_____ 7. Producers have responsibility for overseeing the development of advertisements, so they must be concerned about staying within the client's budget.

Directions For each of the following items, decide which choice best completes the statement. Write the letter that identifies your choice on the answer line.

_____ 8. Which of the following is not a purpose of advertising?
A. deliver a message to a target market
B. sell a specific product or service
C. build a brand
D. all of the above are purposes

_____ 9. _____________ advertising gives the benefits of a specific product or service and relies on rational arguments to explain why a customer should buy it.
A. Product
B. Brand
C. Corporate
D. Image

_____10. The job of the account planner in an advertising agency is to
A. obtain clients
B. learn as much as possible about the target market
C. manage the creative process
D. manage the client's budget

_____11. Associations with a brand such as attitude or personality are called the
A. brand logo
B. brand image
C. brand character
D. brand culture

Activity 1 • Types of Advertising

Directions Evaluate a number of advertisements in a variety of media (television, radio, newspaper, magazine, outdoor, Internet). Identify a good example of a product advertisement, a brand advertisement, and a corporate advertisement. In the spaces below, describe the key information and images of the advertisement. Then discuss why it is an example of the specific type of a advertising.

Product Advertisement

The target market for the advertisement is: ______________________________

____

The key information and images of the advertisement are: ____________________

____

____

____

The advertisement is a good example of product advertising because: ____________

____

____

Brand Advertisement

The target market for the advertisement is: ______________________________

____

The key information and images of the advertisement are: ____________________

____

____

____

The advertisement is a good example of brand advertising because: ______________

____

____

Corporate Advertisement

The target market for the advertisement is: ______________________________

____

The key information and images of the advertisement are: ____________________

____

____

____

The advertisement is a good example of corporate advertising because: ___________

____

____

____

Name ______________________________ Date __________ Class ______________

Lesson 16.2 Plan Advertising

LESSON QUIZ

Directions For each of the following statements, if the statement is true, write a T on the answer line; if the statement is false, write an F on the answer line.

_____ 1. An advertising plan is a document that outlines the activities to be completed and resources needed to create advertising.

_____ 2. An advertising campaign includes a series of related advertisements.

_____ 3. The first step in developing an advertising plan is to develop the creative concept.

_____ 4. The best method of establishing an advertising budget is to spend all of the money you can afford.

_____ 5. Examples of advertising media are television and the Internet.

_____ 6. For most advertising, any type of media will have the same strengths and weaknesses.

_____ 7. The reach is the total number of people who see an advertisement.

Directions For each of the following items, decide which choice best completes the statement. Write the letter that identifies your choice on the answer line.

_____ 8. Each objective in your advertising plan should
A. be measurable
B. identify the primary competitors
C. specify the cost of achieving the objective
D. all of the above

_____ 9. When your advertising budget is determined by the percentage of sales approach, your advertising budget
A. may increase but will never decrease
B. will be determined by your past, current, or projected sales
C. will match that of your competitors
D. cannot be set until the end of the sales period

_____10. The number of times a member of the target audience is exposed to the advertising message is the
A. total audience
B. market share
C. frequency
D. RPI

_____11. Which of the following is not a disadvantage of magazine advertising?
A. high clutter
B. expensive
C. long lead time
D. limited audience

Activity 1 • Advertising Objectives

Directions An advertising objective is made up of several parts: (1) the specific message the plan should communicate, (2) the target audience, and (3) the time period in which the goal should be accomplished. Advertising objectives should be very specific and you must be able to measure the success achieved to know when your goal has been accomplished. Identify the parts of the following objectives.

1. Sell 10 percent more floral arrangements to Plainville residents for Valentine's Day.
   Message:____
   Target Audience:____________________________________
   Time Period:______________________________________
   Measurement Method:__________________________________
   ____

2. Increase purchases of store-branded products by 15 percent compared to national brands in the next six months.
   Message:____
   Target Audience:____________________________________
   Time Period:______________________________________
   Measurement Method:__________________________________
   ____

3. Increase income for the automotive service department by 12 percent next year by encouraging new owners to make four maintenance visits each year.
   Message:____
   Target Audience:____________________________________
   Time Period:______________________________________
   Measurement Method: __________________________________
   ____

Activity 2 • Develop the Plan

Directions As personal computers go through a variety of technological innovations, making older versions obsolete almost as soon as they are sold, the e-waste is piling up, literally, in landfills across the nation. Consumers have begun clamoring for computers that reduce, reuse, and recycle. These "green" computers should be upgradeable, their parts should be interchangeable, and the materials should be nontoxic to the environment and to your home. Your company is introducing a new PC named Green PC Pro. It uses a new containment unit made from renewable materials that allows for upgrades in micro-chips and motherboards while maintaining improved performance and storage attributes found in non-green brands. It is priced 25 percent higher than current brands. Develop an advertising plan for this green PC.

Name ______________________________ Date __________ Class ____________________

Lesson 16.3 Create and Evaluate Advertising

LESSON QUIZ

Directions For each of the following statements, if the statement is true, write a T on the answer line; if the statement is false, write an F on the answer line.

_____ 1. The dramatization creative format revolves around people who use the product in a realistic way to solve a problem.

_____ 2. Humor should not be used in an advertisement because it can easily be misinterpreted.

_____ 3. It is illegal to use advertising in which a company makes a claim of superiority over a competitor.

_____ 4. Because of the expense of advertising, clients may conduct customer research on a creative concept before it is approved.

_____ 5. The creative development and production process begins with a strategic brief.

_____ 6. One way to evaluate the effectiveness of an advertisement is to build in a coupon or rebate.

_____ 7. Advertising is regulated by the Federal Trade Commission and the Federal Communications Commission.

Directions For each of the following items, decide which choice best completes the statement. Write the letter that identifies your choice on the answer line.

_____ 8. "I wish I was an Oscar Mayer wiener" is an example of which type of creative format?
A. image
B. musical
C. testimonial
D. comedy

_____ 9. Collecting data that can be classified into meaningful numerical values is
A. advertising evaluation
B. qualitative research
C. quantitative research
D. impact assessment

_____10. A legal order to discontinue deceptive advertising is a
A. cease-and-desist order
B. stop-action order
C. corrective advertising order
D. competitive challenge

_____10. When McDonald's makes the claim in an advertising that its food is healthier than that found at Wendy's or Burger King, it is making what type of claim?
A. testimonial
B. image
C. competitive
D. product demonstration

Activity 1 • Recall Testing

Directions A large manufacturer of Clean-n-Brite laundry detergent plans to conduct a recall test on an ad that will run in a popular magazine. Two hundred supermarket shoppers representing the target market will be randomly chosen to participate in the research. They will be taken to a research room with comfortable seating, beverages, and snacks and given a copy of the magazine in which the advertisement appears. They will be given no specific directions other than to spend as much time as they want reading the magazine. After they have finished, they will be questioned by a researcher.

Develop seven questions that the researchers could ask the research participants after they have read the magazine to determine their level of recall for the specific advertisement and the impressions they have of the brand.

1. ______________________________

2. ______________________________

3. ______________________________

4. ______________________________

5. ______________________________

6. ______________________________

7. ______________________________

Activity 2 • Analyze Print Advertisements

Directions Choose two advertisements from any print medium and mount them on poster board. Answer the following questions about each ad on separate sheets of paper and attach them to the poster.

1. What is the objective of this ad?
2. Who is the intended target market?
3. What is the format?
4. What makes the ad unique or memorable?
5. How could the effectiveness of the advertisement be evaluated?

Name ______________________________ Date ____________ Class ______________________

Lesson 17.1 The Value of Selling

LESSON QUIZ

Directions For each of the following statements, if the statement is true, write a T on the answer line; if the statement is false, write an F on the answer line.

_____ 1. Selling is part of the promotion element of the marketing mix.

_____ 2. Personal selling is most successful when communicating with a large group of people.

_____ 3. It is appropriate for a salesperson to offer a product that the customer did not originally intend to buy if it is the best match with customer needs.

_____ 4. An advertisement can provide more information than can be included in a sales presentation.

_____ 5. An effective salesperson often meets with the customer several times before making the sale.

_____ 6. A salesperson should inform the company when it is evident that the marketing mix does not satisfy customer needs.

_____ 7. Successful salespeople have the qualities of good managers.

Directions For each of the following items, decide which choice best completes the statement. Write the letter that identifies your choice on the answer line.

_____ 8. __________________ provide(s) the link between the customer and the business.
A. Advertising
B. Promotion
C. Salespeople
D. Profit

_____ 9. Which of these indicates the need for personal selling?
A. products that appeal to large numbers of people
B. products purchased frequently with limited need for decision making
C. customers who expect personal attention and help with decision making
D. all are correct

_____10. Which of these is not one of the areas of personal sales management?
A. self-management
B. customer management
C. information management
D. all are a part of personal sales management

_____11. Which of these is both an advantage and disadvantage of personal selling?
A. cost per customer
B. time
C. control
D. flexibility

Activity 1 • Selling Starts at the Top

Directions A survey of CEOs in 664 fast-growing companies asked how many hours per week they devoted to sales and marketing based on a 60-hour work week. The following results were gathered.

Company Sales	Hours Per Week	Percentage Per Week
Less than \$1 million	23	
\$1 million–\$5 million	16	
\$5 million–\$10 million	15	
\$10 million–\$15 million	15	
\$15 million–\$20 million	17	
\$20 million–\$40 million	15	
More than \$40 million	17	

1. Complete the column in the chart that identifies the percentage of time spent on sales and marketing each week.
2. What is the average number of hours per week for all companies?_______________
3. What is the average percentage of hours for companies under \$15 million in sales?_________
4. Draw a bar graph illustrating the percentage of hours spent on sales and marketing.

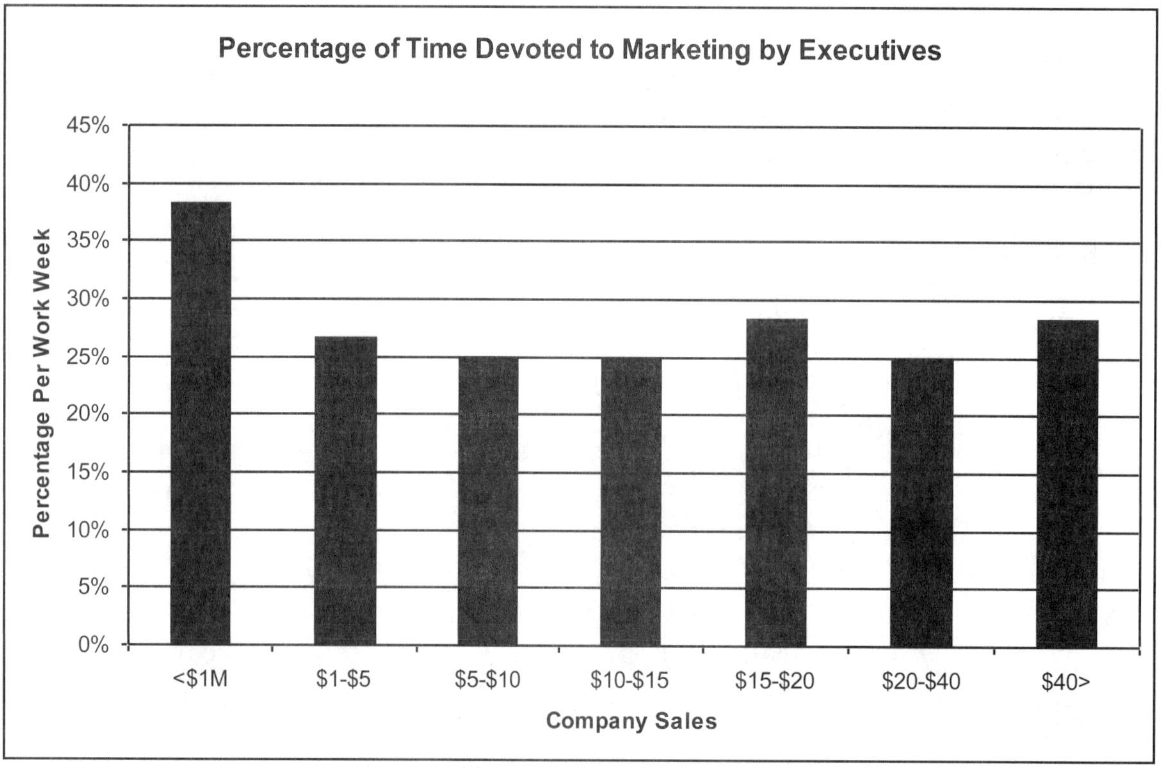

5. From this survey, what conclusions can you draw about the importance of sales and marketing to an organization?____

____

____

Name ______________________________ Date __________ Class ______________________

Lesson 17.2 Prepare for Effective Selling

LESSON QUIZ

Directions For each of the following statements, if the statement is true, write a T on the answer line; if the statement is false, write an F on the answer line.

_____ 1. Effective selling requires a great deal of preparation before the salesperson meets with a customer.

_____ 2. Consumers contacted by salespeople may be upset if they are not expecting the call and are not interested in the products the salesperson is selling.

_____ 3. A marketing-oriented company typically uses cold-calling as the most effective method to contact prospective customers in its target market.

_____ 4. Qualifying involves gathering information to see which consumers are most likely to buy.

_____ 5. It is not necessary to get a customer's full attention and interest until late in the sales presentation.

_____ 6. Every customer experiences a different series of mental stages when making a decision to purchase.

_____ 7. A benefit is the advantage provided to a customer as a result of a product feature.

Directions For each of the following items, decide which choice best completes the statement. Write the letter that identifies your choice on the answer line.

_____ 8. A qualified prospective customer should have
A. a need for the product
B. the resources to purchase the product
C. the authority to make a purchase decision
D. all of the above

_____ 9. Salespeople can gather important information from advertisements, trade shows, and product manuals to understand
A. the customer decision-making process
B. the products and services they sell
C. individual customer needs
D. all of the above

_____10. When presenting information to customers about competitors' products and services, a salesperson should
A. present only general or obvious information
B. make negative comments
C. avoid any mention of competitors
D. carefully and accurately compare advantages and disadvantages

Activity 1 • Information Is Money

Directions The right information can help a salesperson close a sale. Choose a product for which customers make a careful decision and usually purchase from a salesperson. Research each of the following categories of information related to that product that would help you make an effective sales presentation. Record the information you obtained in the space provided.

Product's marketing mix: ______________________________

Target market characteristics, needs, and decision-making process: ______________________________

Competition: ______________________________

Features/benefits and main selling points: ______________________________

Name ______________________________ Date __________ Class ____________________

Lesson 17.3 The Selling Process and Sales Support

LESSON QUIZ

Directions For each of the following statements, if the statement is true, write a T on the answer line; if the statement is false, write an F on the answer line.

_____ 1. People who are skilled at selling are in high demand in business.

_____ 2. During the preapproach, salespeople study information available on specific customers.

_____ 3. The approach may be initiated either by the salesperson or the customer.

_____ 4. The approach in retail selling is the same process as used by business-to-business salespeople.

_____ 5. If a salesperson demonstrates a feature very well, there will be no need to describe the benefit of that feature to the customer.

_____ 6. If a customer asks questions during a product demonstration, it is evidence the salesperson is not communicating effectively.

_____ 7. Even though distribution of products occurs after the sale is made, salespeople still need to understand the distribution activities used to get the product to the customer.

Directions For each of the following items, decide which choice best completes the statement. Write the letter that identifies your choice on the answer line.

_____ 8. An inappropriate way to attempt to close a sale is to
A. offer the customer a choice
B. review an important benefit
C. suggest this may be the last item in stock
D. ask about the method of payment preferred by the customer

_____ 9. Offering additional support and services after the initial sale in order to increase customer satisfaction is known as
A. suggestion selling
B. follow-up
C. cold calling
D. sales support

_____10. A benefit of follow-up with customers after a sale is
A. it provides another opportunity to reinforce the customer's decision
B. it determines if the customer has additional unsatisfied needs
C. it may lead to referrals of additional customers
D. all are benefits

_____11. The preapproach is included in which step of the selling process?
A. determine needs
B. demonstrate product
C. answer customer questions
D. the approach

Activity 1 • Features and Benefits

Directions Customers are impressed by benefits rather than features. They want to know what the feature can do for them. For each feature described below, identify the benefit it provides for the customer.

Feature	Benefit
Anti-lock brakes on an automobile	
Automatic timer on a coffeemaker	
Flat-screen computer monitor	
Stainless steel components	
Adjustable waistband on men's slacks	
Brick exterior for a home	
Double-sided copying on a printer	
Furniture fabrics available in a variety of colors	
Luggage with wheels and a collapsible handle	
Flexible neck on a work light	

Activity 2 • Job Search

Directions Every week, businesses advertise positions for professional salespeople who will sell the company's products and services to other businesses. Use your most recent Sunday newspaper or one of the job sites on the Internet. Record the information in the chart below for two advertised business-to-business sales positions.

Title/Company	Job Description	Amount of Travel	Type of Compensation

Name ______________________ Date __________ Class ______________

Lesson 18.1 The Expanding World Economy

LESSON QUIZ

Directions For each of the following statements, if the statement is true, write a T on the answer line; if the statement is false, write an F on the answer line.

_____ 1. Most of the products and services produced in the world are consumed by the people in the countries where they are produced.

_____ 2. The United States has the second largest economy in the world behind only the European Union.

_____ 3. Years ago, raw materials made up almost all of the products traded between countries.

_____ 4. International trade in services is growing faster than trade in products.

_____ 5. One reason businesses get involved in international competition is that they can't find adequate competition in their home markets.

_____ 6. The process of international trade is difficult, so international trade has declined.

_____ 7. Many states have trade promotion offices to help businesses develop markets in other countries.

Directions For each of the following items, decide which choice best completes the statement. Write the letter that identifies your choice on the answer line.

_____ 8. Products and services sold to another country are
A. imports
B. excess inventory
C. exports
D. all of the above

_____ 9. Some businesspeople may choose not to become involved in international trade because
A. selling products in other countries appears to be complicated
B. international laws do not encourage trade between countries
C. most foreign consumers prefer products produced in their own countries
D. only very large and experienced businesses can be successful in international trade

_____10. The government provides support for U.S. businesses through
A. embassies in most countries
B. the Small Business Administration
C. the U.S. Department of Commerce
D. all of the above

Activity 1 • Exports and Imports

Directions The amount of exports and imports varies considerably from country to country. Use the library or Internet to find the most recent information on the dollar value of exports and imports for each of the countries to complete the table below.

Country	Exports (mil.)	Imports (mil.)	Country	Exports (mil.)	Imports (mil.)
Israel	$	$	Argentina	$	$
Ireland			Bangladesh		
Austria			Belgium		
Uganda			Bolivia		
Hungary			Brazil		
India			Canada		
Egypt			China		
Sudan			Cuba		
New Zealand			Denmark		
Singapore			France		
Malaysia			Germany		
Ecuador			Guatemala		
Norway			Italy		
Zambia			Kenya		
Pakistan			Mexico		
Peru			Morocco		
Switzerland			Poland		
Russia			Sweden		
Japan			Uganda		

Activity 2 • Export Products

Directions Select one of the countries identified in the previous activity other than the United States. Identify the major products and materials the country currently exports and imports.

Country :____

Exports: ____

____

Imports: ____

____

Name ______________________________________ Date ___________ Class ______________________

Lesson 18.2 How Businesses Get Involved

LESSON QUIZ

Directions For each of the following statements, if the statement is true, write a T on the answer line; if the statement is false, write an F on the answer line.

_____ 1. A company involved in indirect exporting sells products to a business in one country where they are then exported to a second country.

_____ 2. A negative balance of trade demonstrates that businesses from other countries are satisfying the needs of consumers better than the country's own businesses.

_____ 3. In 2013, the United States was the world's leading importer and exporter.

_____ 4. With foreign production, a company owns and operates production facilities in its home country and exports them to other countries.

_____ 5. The United States is an attractive country in which foreign businesses like to invest.

_____ 6. Multinational companies have operations throughout the world and conduct planning for worldwide markets.

_____ 7. Multinational companies generally compete with the same set of competitors in every country where they sell their product and services.

Directions For each of the following items, decide which choice best completes the statement. Write the letter that identifies your choice on the answer line.

_____ 8. The difference between the amount of a country's imports and exports is its
A. gross domestic product
B. gross national product
C. foreign investments
D. balance of trade

_____ 9. When independent companies develop a relationship to participate in common business activities, this is known as
A. a foreign investment
B. a multinational company
C. a joint venture
D. normal business operations

_____10. A foreign investment occurs when
A. a consumer purchases a product manufactured in another country
B. an existing business in another country is purchased
C. products are manufactured in another country
D. someone in another country purchases an item made in the United States

Activity 1 • Currency Exchange

Directions Every day, products and services from one country are sold in other countries. The sale often requires converting the currency of the buyer to that of the seller. Currency exchange rates are established by international financial institutions to determine the value of each currency. Locate a currency exchange converter on the Internet and use the converter to complete the following table with the most recent currency exchange data. Then, use the information to answer the questions that follow.

	U.S. Dollar	Bahrain Dinar	Brazil Real	Canada Dollar	Germany Euro	India Rupee	Japan Yen	South Africa Rand	United Kingdom Pound
U.S. Dollar	1								
Bahrain Dinar		1							
Brazil Real			1						
Canada Dollar				1					
Germany Euro					1				
India Rupee						1			
Japan Yen							1		
South Africa Rand								1	
United Kingdom Pound									1

1. Juniper Inc. in Canada purchased 16 planes from an American company for $415,000 each in U.S. dollars. How much did the company pay in Canada dollars? ____________________
2. My Maps in Brazil purchased 150 maps from a German company for a total of 525 German Euros. How much did the company pay in Brazil Real? ____________________
3. Sherman Auto Parts in the United States purchased a diesel engine from a Bahrain company for 3,628,000 Bahrain Dinar. How much did the company pay in U.S. dollars? ____________________
4. Faster Flycycles in South Africa purchased 1,200 bicycles from an India company for 720 Rupees each. How much did the company pay in South Africa Rands? ____________________

Name ______________________________ Date __________ Class ____________________

Lesson 18.3 Understand International Markets

LESSON QUIZ

Directions For each of the following statements, if the statement is true, write a T on the answer line; if the statement is false, write an F on the answer line.

_____ 1. The concept of a market in other countries is the same as the concept of a market in the United States.

_____ 2. It is not necessary to develop a unique marketing mix to sell products in another country.

_____ 3. Preindustrial countries most often export manufactured goods.

_____ 4. Today, most countries have postindustrial economies.

_____ 5. A country's gross domestic product is the same as its gross national product

_____ 6. An increasing standard of living is a sign of a strong economy because more jobs are available and wages are increasing.

_____ 7. Quotas are limits on the numbers of specific types of products that foreign companies can sell in the country.

Directions For each of the following items, decide which choice best completes the statement. Write the letter that identifies your choice on the answer line.

_____ 8. Countries with postindustrial economies
A. have a mix of business and consumer products produced and marketed in the global marketplace
B. have a high standard of living
C. work with other countries to develop laws and procedures to encourage and support international trade
D. all of the above

_____ 9. A country's purchasing power decreases
A. as a result of inflation
B. if its standard of living increases
C. if productivity increases
D. all of the above

_____10. When adjusting a marketing mix for a product to be sold in an international market, a company should
A. not change the product or service
B. make sure their representatives understand the customs and culture of the country
C. use a bank in its home country rather than a foreign bank
D. avoid using the Internet because it is not well developed in most other countries

Activity 1 • Export Gum to the United States

Directions Assume you are a foreign exporter planning to introduce a new brand and flavor of chewing gum to the United States. Using your knowledge of U.S. markets, complete the following chart of marketing functions to describe what you would do to bring your product here.

Marketing Function	Description of Activities
Market Planning	
Product and Service Management	
Marketing-Information Management	
Selling	
Financing	
Promotion	
Risk Management	
Distribution	
Pricing	

Name ________________________________ Date __________ Class ____________________

Lesson 19.1 Assess Business Risks

LESSON QUIZ

Directions For each of the following statements, if the statement is true, write a T on the answer line; if the statement is false, write an F on the answer line.

_____ 1. People invest time and money in new businesses or products when there is a risk of loss because there is also an opportunity for success and profit.

_____ 2. Success in marketing is always determined by profit.

_____ 3. Every business faces risks, but individual consumers do not.

_____ 4. A pure risk presents the possibility of an opportunity for gain but not loss.

_____ 5. If your actions can affect the possibility of a risk, it is a controllable risk.

_____ 6. An example of a speculative risk would be the stock market.

_____ 7. People responsible for risk management go through a careful process to decide the best way to deal with each risk the business faces.

Directions For each of the following items, decide which choice best completes the statement. Write the letter that identifies your choice on the answer line.

_____ 8. A risk that is faced by a large number of people, is pure rather than speculative, and has a predictable amount of loss is a(n)
A. insurable risk
B. controlled risk
C. pure risk
D. natural risk

_____ 9. Areas prone to earthquakes pose a(n) ____________ risk for companies located there.
A. insurable
B. controlled
C. pure
D. natural

_____10. If a business chooses to let another business complete a risky activity for it, the business is
A. transferring the risk
B. avoiding the risk
C. assuming the risk
D. insuring the risk

_____11. A company that assumes a risk
A. purchases insurance to protect the company from the loss
B. sues the company or individual responsible for any loss
C. faces the risk and deals with the result
D. all of the above

Activity 1 • Types of Risk

Directions For each of the following statements, determine the type of risk in each category.

Event	Type of Risk		
	Pure (P)/ Speculative (S)	Controllable (C)/ Uncontrollable (U)	Insurable (I)/ Uninsurable (U)
An electrical outage causes the food in your store's freezers to spoil.			
A hailstorm destroys more than half of your vegetable crop.			
You install mirrors on the ends of the aisles in your store to detect shoplifters.			
A country to which you export your product places new tariffs on incoming products.			
The FDA releases a report that a chemical you use in your manufacturing process might be considered harmful.			

Activity 2 • Shoplifting and Employee Theft

Directions The owner of a clothing store in a shopping mall estimates that approximately 2 percent of gross sales are lost to shoplifters and employee theft. From your knowledge of risk management and business practices, describe at least three actions the manager might take for each of these problems.

Shoplifting: ____

____

____

____

Employee theft: ____

____

____

____

Name ____ Date ____________ Class__________________________

Lesson 19.2 Identify Marketing Risks

LESSON QUIZ

Directions For each of the following statements, if the statement is true, write a T on the answer line; if the statement is false, write an F on the answer line.

_____ 1. Risk management is an important part of the product/service management function.

_____ 2. Marketers evaluate opportunities to determine which provide the greatest opportunities with the least risk.

_____ 3. Competitors' actions cannot be predicted so should not be considered a business risk.

_____ 4. Packaging a product presents very little risk to a company.

_____ 5. Some elements of the marketing mix are not subject to risks.

_____ 6. The greatest risk businesses face for the product mix element is liability.

_____ 7. Businesses cannot be held liable legally for inaccurate or misleading advertising.

Directions For each of the following items, decide which choice best completes the statement. Write the letter that identifies your choice on the answer line.

_____ 8. Providing security and safety for products, personnel, and customers and reducing the risk associated with marketing decisions and activities is
A. marketing management
B. market opportunity analysis
C. liability analysis
D. risk management

_____ 9. A legal responsibility for loss or damage is
A. shoplifting
B. risk
C. liability
D. insurance

_____10. Which of the following examples illustrates a risk in the distribution mix element?
A. A competitor introduces a new product.
B. Products can be stolen by burglars, shoplifters, or employees.
C. A new electronic billboard is installed directly across from your business sponsored by your main competitor.
D. All of the above are correct.

_____11. An out-of-date product may lead to which of the following risks?
A. product design risk
B. risk of damage
C. liability risk
D. performance risk

Activity 1 • Risk Management with the Channel of Distribution

Directions Distribution channel members are instrumental in minimizing and often assuming risks for the manufacturer and retailer. Answer the question posed in column one for the three types of businesses in columns two, three, and four.

Question	Retailer of Fresh Vegetables	Wholesaler of Office Supplies	Real Estate Agent
What characteristics of the product will be affected by risk?			
What services or activities must be provided in order to minimize risk?			
Who will be responsible for the distribution?			
Who assumes the risk?			

Activity 2 • Analyze Risk to Improve Exchanges

Directions You are the manager of a convenience store. Your district manager has given you a checklist of areas where attention to risks can improve satisfying exchanges with customers. List at least two measures you can take to manage risk for each area of concern.

Area of Concern	Risk Management Measures
Customer Safety	
Employee Safety	
Marketing Mix	

Name ____ Date ____________ Class ______________________

Lesson 19.3 Manage Marketing Risks

LESSON QUIZ

Directions For each of the following statements, if the statement is true, write a T on the answer line; if the statement is false, write an F on the answer line.

_____ 1. The first goal of risk management should be to reduce the negative effects of risks on the business and its customers.

_____ 2. A business should always choose the marketing mix alternative that has the least amount of risk.

_____ 3. Risk reduction activities and responsibilities should be identified in the marketing plan.

_____ 4. All marketing personnel should receive training in safety and security procedures.

_____ 5. Life insurance for a company's top marketing executive is an example of professional liability insurance.

_____ 6. With careful planning, all of the major risks a business faces can be eliminated.

_____ 7. The careful selection of marketing personnel is actually a method of reducing risks.

Directions For each of the following items, decide which choice best completes the statement. Write the letter that identifies your choice on the answer line.

_____ 8. A market analysis should identify
- A. insurance requirements for a business
- B. marketing mixes that have no risks
- C. specific activities the company should take to reduce risks
- D. the risks and opportunities that relate to competitors' actions

_____ 9. A responsibility of the marketing manager is to carefully review each part of the action plan to
- A. establish marketing goals
- B. determine if risks are adequately addressed
- C. cut costs
- D. proofread the plan for errors

_____10. Purchasing insurance is a method of
- A. transferring risk
- B. establishing a marketing strategy
- C. addressing customer needs
- D. all of the above

_____11. Which of these marketing plan sections does not provide an opportunity to identify and develop plans for managing risks?
- A. Market Analysis
- B. Marketing Strategy
- C. Action Plan
- D. Executive Summary

Activity 1 • Risks and Opportunities

Directions Risks and opportunities are a part of all businesses and can be found in each of the marketing functions. Select a business in your community. Carefully analyze the business using each of the nine marketing functions. For each marketing function identify one risk the business may face and one opportunity available to the business that is specifically related to that function. Compare your answers with those of other students who have analyzed a different business.

Business: ____

Marketing Function	Risk Facing the Business	Opportunity Available to the Business
Market Planning		
Product and Service Management		
Selling		
Financing		
Promotion		
Risk Management		
Distribution		
Pricing		
Marketing-Information Management		

Name ______________________________ Date __________ Class ______________________

Lesson 20.1 Marketing Affects Business Finances

LESSON QUIZ

Directions For each of the following statements, if the statement is true, write a T on the answer line; if the statement is false, write an F on the answer line.

_____ 1. Marketing costs have little effect on the overall profitability of a business.

_____ 2. Much of the revenue generated by a business results from marketing activities—the sale of products and services.

_____ 3. Finances are important even to nonprofit organizations.

_____ 4. When marketers consider changes in the marketing mix, they need to study the costs of the changes and predict the effect on sales.

_____ 5. Short-term expenses are for items used within a short time, typically five years or less.

_____ 6. Most of the long-term expenses of a business are directly related to marketing activities.

_____ 7. The costs of day-to-day marketing activities are considered operating expenses.

Directions For each of the following items, decide which choice best completes the statement. Write the letter that identifies your choice on the answer line.

_____ 8. The basic financial equation is:
A. Profit or Loss = Revenues − Costs
B. Total Expenses = Long-Term Expenses − Short-Term Expenses
C. Profit or Loss = Revenue + Expenses
D. Profit or Loss = Capital − Operating Expenses

_____ 9. Although most large organizations have departments that deal specifically with financial planning and management, marketers
A. are still responsible for the revenues and expenses related to marketing
B. need to find ways to increase revenues while controlling costs
C. must identify target markets that provide the most profitable opportunities
D. all of the above

_____10. Long-term expenses usually include
A. advertising and promotion
B. salaries and wages
C. equipment and buildings
D. none of the above

_____11. Which of the following is not a common way for businesses to finance inventory?
A. pay cash each time inventory is ordered
B. obtain short-term loans from financial institutions
C. use credit extended by the seller
D. all are common ways

Activity 1 • New Opportunities for Revenues and Expenses

Directions Trina and Pao have been mowing lawns on a part-time basis all through high school. Over the winter when business is slow, they are trying to brainstorm a list of new services to offer. They realize that additional services increase both revenue and expenses. Help Trina and Pao by completing the following table. The first item is completed for you.

New Services	Additional Expenses
Seeding new lawns	*New equipment for seeding, fertilizing, and watering; costs to purchase seed and fertilizer; credit expenses for new purchases; storage cost of additional materials and equipment; equipment maintenance*
Maintaining shrubs	
Offering credit	
Winter snow removal from sidewalks and driveways	

Activity 2 • Categorize Expenses

Directions Big City Lights is a specialty store offering lighting products and fixtures such as lamps, ceiling lights, garden lights, and other lighting used for homes and offices. The owner plans to open another store in the near future. Complete the following table by analyzing the list of expenses. The first item is completed for you.

Expense	Long Term (L) or Short Term (S)	Capital (C), Inventory (I), or Operating (O)
Building		
Salaries for additional employees		
Computer to track sales and inventory		
Delivery van		
Monthly flyers for advertising		
Office supplies		
Employee training		
Electricity and telephone expenses		
New line of home lighting products		

Name ______________________________ Date __________ Class ____________________

Lesson 20.2 Tools For Financial Planning

LESSON QUIZ

Directions For each of the following statements, if the statement is true, write a T on the answer line; if the statement is false, write an F on the answer line.

_____ 1. Financial forecasts are numerical predictions of future performance related to revenue and expenses.

_____ 2. Businesses have found that most long-term financial forecasts for five years or more can be very accurate.

_____ 3. The most important financial forecasts for marketers are sales, market share, and marketing expenses.

_____ 4. Businesses normally develop a single marketing budget to cover all products, markets, and major marketing activities.

_____ 5. The purpose of an income statement is to determine if the business earned a profit or loss on its operations during a specific period of time.

_____ 6. When managers identify the activities that must be completed to accomplish the goals of the business, they develop budgets to anticipate the costs of those activities.

_____ 7. Marketers should be concerned about ways to increase sales and revenues rather than how to control marketing costs.

Directions For each of the following items, decide which choice best completes the statement. Write the letter that identifies your choice on the answer line.

_____ 8. A detailed projection of financial performance for a specific time period, usually a year or less, is a
A. forecast
B. budget
C. market share prediction
D. sales projection

_____ 9. Today most of the financial information related to marketing activities is collected
A. by employees recording information as they complete the activities
B. from customer records
C. using scanners and computer database technology
D. by counting inventory and cash register receipts

_____10. The most common financial planning method is to
A. use information from comparable businesses and markets
B. look for related figures that help to predict performance
C. use past performance
D. examine the financial plans of competitors

Activity 1 • Before and After

Directions The EconAll Drug Store planned a major promotional campaign to celebrate its one-year anniversary. After the promotion was over, management reviewed the financial information to compare budgeted and actual amounts. The information is provided in the following table.

Promotion Expense	Forecast	Actual	Difference
Television	$12,350	$13,500	
Radio	3,440	2,990	
Print	5,000	5,000	
Coupons	1,500	900	
Give-aways	6,500	7,350	
Additional Wages	4,500	6,500	
Total	$33,290	$36,240	

1. Complete the table by calculating the dollar difference between the forecast and actual money spent.
2. The store's annual promotional budget is $150,000. What percentage of the total budget was used for this promotional campaign? ______________________________
3. The store anticipated that the budgeted promotional expenses would be 18% of the store sales for the two-week period. The actual sales were $223,550.

   What was the projected amount of sales?______________________________

   What percentage of actual sales was spent on the promotional campaign?______________

Activity 2 • Planning with Marketing Information Systems

Directions Marketing information management systems play a significant role in capturing and storing information to be used later for financial planning and analysis. To help in developing each of the following reports, list several types of information that should be maintained in the company's marketing information system.

Sales Forecast: ______________________________

____

Market Share: ______________________________

____

Customer Accounts: ______________________________

____

Income Statement: ______________________________

____

Name ______________________________ Date ____________ Class ______________________

Lesson 20.3 Budget For Marketing Activities

LESSON QUIZ

Directions For each of the following statements, if the statement is true, write a T on the answer line; if the statement is false, write an F on the answer line.

_____ 1. The basis for developing a marketing budget is a marketing strategy.

_____ 2. A marketing plan describes the marketing activities to be completed and the resources needed.

_____ 3. The primary objective of a marketing strategy is for the business to obtain the most profitable level of sales possible while satisfying a target market.

_____ 4. Prospective customers are normally more profitable than current customers.

_____ 5. If credit is offered to customers, the sale is not complete until the customer pays for the purchase.

_____ 6. Implementing some of the marketing mix elements may not involve any expenses.

_____ 7. Offering satisfied customers money or other incentives if they identify a prospective customer who then buys a product is a promotional expense.

Directions For each of the following items, decide which choice best completes the statement. Write the letter that identifies your choice on the answer line.

_____ 8. Sources of revenue affected by marketing activities include all of the following except
A. initial purchases by customers
B. purchases of products and services by customers after the initial sale is complete
C. interest from credit sales
D. all are marketing-related revenue sources

_____ 9. Replacing a product because it is damaged or does not meet customers' needs
A. reduces the amount of revenue from sales
B. reduces customer satisfaction
C. reduces distribution costs
D. all of the above

_____10. The major expense to a company offering credit to customers is
A. the cost of advertising the product or service
B. the cost making markups and markdowns
C. the cost of uncollected accounts
D. the cost of inventory

_____11. Which of these is not an example of after-sale revenue?
A. an auto dealership servicing and repairing the vehicles it sells
B. a store accepting credit for purchases
C. a theater selling popcorn and soft drinks
D. sale of T-shirts and CDs at a concert venue

Activity 1 • Demonstrate Financial Skills

Directions Marketers must be able to understand and use financial statements. Use the following information to prepare an income statement in the space below. Then, in the last column, calculate percentages to compare gross sales with net sales, cost of goods sold, gross margin, total expenses, and net income.

Gross sales, $175,392.36; returns, $1,587.34; beginning inventory, $49,222.43; purchases, $76,234.76; ending inventory, $25,768.45. Expenses for operating the business: salaries, $31,394.22; licenses, $2,547.45; rent, $6,000; advertising, $25,000; professional services, $600; insurance, $1,200; telephone, $1,254.36; postage, $769.33; and utilities, $2,688.67.

INCOME STATEMENT

For the three-month period ending ___________

			Percentages
REVENUE:			
Gross sales			
Returns			
Net sales			
Beginning inventory			
Purchases			
Cost of goods for sale			
Ending inventory			
Cost of goods sold			
Gross margin			
EXPENSES:			
Salaries			
Licenses			
Rent			
Advertising			
Professional services			
Insurance			
Telephone			
Postage			
Utilities			
Total expenses			
NET INCOME			

Name ______________________________ Date __________ Class ____________________

Lesson 21.1 Understand Entrepreneurship

LESSON QUIZ

Directions For each of the following statements, if the statement is true, write a T on the answer line; if the statement is false, write an F on the answer line.

_____ 1. Two important reasons people start their own business is to have the freedom to do work that they enjoy and to take responsibility for the success or failure of the business.

_____ 2. Anyone who owns a business is considered to be an entrepreneur.

_____ 3. More than 10 percent of the working population in the United States is self-employed.

_____ 4. Small businesses make up more than 97 percent of all businesses in the United States.

_____ 5. An advantage of entrepreneurship is that the owner typically works fewer hours than does the average employee in a business.

_____ 6. Most entrepreneurs start their first business while still working for another company.

_____ 7. Most entrepreneurs do not want their businesses to grow to the point where they have to hire additional employees.

Directions For each of the following items, decide which choice best completes the statement. Write the letter that identifies your choice on the answer line.

_____ 8. Someone who takes the risk to start a new business is known as
A. a small business owner
B. an investor
C. an entrepreneur
D. a franchisor

_____ 9. Entrepreneurs start which type of businesses?
A. production
B. manufacturing
C. retail and service
D. all of the above

_____10. Which of these statements is not true about small businesses in the United States?
A. They employ more than 50 percent of all non-government employees.
B. They employ fewer than 30 percent of all workers in high-tech occupations.
C. They provide about 75 percent of all new jobs.
D. They are responsible for more than half of all goods and services produced.

_____11. Small business are more likely to hire
A. younger workers
B. older workers
C. workers who need part-time jobs
D. all of the above

Activity 1 • The Stories of Entrepreneurs

Directions Many entrepreneurs started with a small dream that became a success story that affected the lives of many investors, employees, and consumers. Well-known entrepreneurs include Henry Ford, Bill Gates, Madame C. J. Walker, Levi Strauss, Russell Simmons, Ben Cohen, Jerry Yang, Richard Branson, Andrew Carnegie, and Oprah Winfrey, to name a few. Select two entrepreneurs—one who started a business more than 50 years ago and one who started a business in the past 20 years. Use the library or Internet to gather information on each entrepreneur to answer the following questions. If possible locate a picture of the entrepreneur and his or her product or business.

Entrepreneur: ______________________ Product or Business: ______________________

Date of birth: __________________ Year the first business was started: __________________

Brief personal history and personal characteristics: ______________________________

____

____

Description of the business and its history: ______________________________

____

____

Impact on the industry, economy, and consumers: ______________________________

____

____

Personal philosophy about business and entrepreneurship: ______________________

____

Entrepreneur: ______________________ Product or Business: ______________________

Date of birth: __________________ Year the first business was started: __________________

Brief personal history and personal characteristics: ______________________________

____

____

Description of the business and its history: ______________________________

____

____

Impact on the industry, economy, and consumers: ______________________________

____

____

Personal philosophy about business and entrepreneurship: ______________________

____

Name ______________________________ Date __________ Class ______________

Lesson 21.2 Characteristics of Entrepreneurs

LESSON QUIZ

Directions For each of the following statements, if the statement is true, write a T on the answer line; if the statement is false, write an F on the answer line.

_____ 1. With the desire and will, almost anyone can become an entrepreneur.

_____ 2. The typical entrepreneur enjoys team activities and cooperates well with others.

_____ 3. You can be a small business owner without being an entrepreneur.

_____ 4. Gaining business experience is an important part of preparing to become a successful entrepreneur.

_____ 5. Most of the people who start successful businesses today have completed high school and often have one or more college degrees.

_____ 6. Entrepreneurs often work for another company for many years before starting their own businesses.

_____ 7. Many entrepreneurs suffer business failures before succeeding.

Directions For each of the following items, decide which choice best completes the statement. Write the letter that identifies your choice on the answer line.

_____ 8. To become a successful entrepreneur, your academic preparation should include
A. technological skills
B. communication skills
C. math skills
D. all of these

_____ 9. Taking science classes will help you learn to
A. solve problems
B. conduct research
C. make decisions based on analytical procedures
D. all of these

_____10. The informal code of conduct regarding acceptable online behavior is known as
A. blogging
B. netiquette
C. business etiquette
D. an emoticon

_____11. All of the following are characteristics of entrepreneurs except
A. entrepreneurs are risk-averse
B. entrepreneurs are creative
C. entrepreneurs are self-confident
D. entrepreneurs are independent

Activity 1 • Prepare for Entrepreneurship

Directions Every entrepreneur is a unique individual, even though he or she may share common characteristics. Rate yourself on a scale of 1 (low) to 10 (high) for the entrepreneurial characteristics listed below and explain why you have given yourself that rating.

Focused and goal-oriented: 1 2 3 4 5 6 7 8 9 10

Explanation: ______________________________

____

Risk taking: 1 2 3 4 5 6 7 8 9 10

Explanation: ______________________________

____

Desire to achieve: 1 2 3 4 5 6 7 8 9 10

Explanation: ______________________________

Independence: 1 2 3 4 5 6 7 8 9 10

Explanation: ______________________________

____

Self-confidence: 1 2 3 4 5 6 7 8 9 10

Explanation: ______________________________

Creativity: 1 2 3 4 5 6 7 8 9 10

Explanation: ______________________________

Number of items rated 1–5 ________ Number of items rated 6–10 ________

What specific things can you do while in high school to prepare for entrepreneurship?

____

____

____

____

Name ______________________________ Date __________ Class ______________

Lesson 21.3 Business Ownership Opportunities

LESSON QUIZ

Directions For each of the following statements, if the statement is true, write a T on the answer line; if the statement is false, write an F on the answer line.

_____ 1. Entrepreneurship includes business opportunities as diverse as farming and fitness centers.

_____ 2. Each of the marketing functions provides entrepreneurship opportunities.

_____ 3. Consumer credit provides low-value loans to people who cannot qualify for traditional bank loans.

_____ 4. Entrepreneurship opportunities exist for helping companies with risk-management activities such as providing security services.

_____ 5. In choosing a potential business opportunity, an entrepreneur's only consideration should be that he or she likes the business and has the interests and skills to operate it successfully.

_____ 6. Identifying a target market before starting a new business actually reduces the chances for an entrepreneur's success.

_____ 7. Disposal of products offers many opportunities for entrepreneurs including recovering raw materials from landfills, recycling, and developing ideas for obsolete products.

Directions For each of the following items, decide which choice best completes the statement. Write the letter that identifies your choice on the answer line.

_____ 8. Retailers and wholesalers are marketing businesses because they
A. earn a profit
B. participate in the exchange process between producers and consumers
C. actually create products and services
D. all of the above

_____ 9. A promotional approach that encourages people to pass along marketing messages through word-of-mouth, creating a rapid dissemination of information is known as
A. viral marketing
B. virus marketing
C. Internet marketing
D. word-of-mouth promotion

_____10. A new business will have difficulty competing with existing businesses unless those businesses
A. have more customers than they want
B. have weaknesses in their operations or marketing strategies
C. begin offering new products or services
D. reduce their prices

Activity 1 • Turn Skills into Businesses

Directions Many skills can be turned into a unique business. Complete the following table. Describe a unique business that can be created from the skill identified on the left. Identify which of the businesses are marketing businesses by writing yes or no in the last column.

Skill	Unique Business	Marketing or Not?
Drawing		
Research		
Physical Fitness		
Computer Skills		
Speaking		
Teaching		
Poetry		
Fishing		
Math		

Activity 2 • Compare the Competition

Directions Select a business that you visit frequently. Assume you want to establish a business that will compete with the existing business. Answer the following questions to aid you with your planning.

Strengths of the existing business: ____________________

____

Weaknesses of the existing business: ____________________

____

How your target market will be similar or different: ____________________

____

How your marketing mix will be similar or different: ____________________

____

Name ______________________ Date __________ Class ______________

Lesson 21.4 Legal Needs of Entrepreneurs

LESSON QUIZ

Directions For each of the following statements, if the statement is true, write a T on the answer line; if the statement is false, write an F on the answer line.

_____ 1. Because entrepreneurs are the sole owners of their businesses, they must organize as a proprietorship.

_____ 2. The corporation is the most common form of business ownership, with nearly three-quarters of all businesses organized in this way.

_____ 3. Banks are more likely to loan money to partnerships than to proprietorships.

_____ 4. A corporation is able to operate as if it were a person in that it can borrow money, enter into contracts, and is liable for its decisions and actions.

_____ 5. With a corporation an entrepreneur should always take responsibility for day-to-day management activities.

_____ 6. Businesses formed by entrepreneurs do not need to file for patents, trademarks, or copyrights.

_____ 7. An entrepreneur risks failure if he or she does not seek legal advice when starting a new business.

Directions For each of the following items, decide which choice best completes the statement. Write the letter that identifies your choice on the answer line.

_____ 8. A legal document that specifies the responsibilities and financial relationships of the partners is a(n)
A. partnership agreement
B. charter
C. ownership agreement
D. business plan

_____ 9. Advantages of a corporation include
A. if money is owed, there is no need to pay the debt
B. most states do not require a charter to be filed
C. the business continues to operate even if one owner decides to sell all of his or her stock
D. owners do not have to provide any money in order to start the business

_____10. Legal steps for starting a business include
A. register the name of your new business
B. prepare to collect and report all local, state, and federal taxes
C. obtain financing for purchases and business operations
D. all of the above

Activity 1 • Business Names Have Meaning

Directions The name of a business can create an image for potential customers. Create a name for each business described in the table below. Provide a brief description of why you believe the name is particularly appealing to the specific target market.

Description	Name	Why is it appealing?
Offers in-home puppy training for families with small children		
Provides interior decorating services for new homeowners on a low budget		
Creates ice sculptures for weddings, parties, and other celebrations		
Provides unique exterior paint jobs for used cars to fit the owner's personality		
Offers personalized vacation planning to out-of-the-way parts of the world		
Offers emergency online homework help for middle school and high school students		

Activity 2 • Public Corporations from Small Businesses

Directions Many corporations were started by entrepreneurs but are now large publicly traded companies in which you can invest. Use an online service that provides company descriptions and investment information. Choose a publicly traded company that was started by an entrepreneur and answer the following questions.

Name of company: ______________________ Name of founder: ______________________

Stock symbol: ______ Current stock price: ______ Year high and low: ______________________

Product or service: ______________________ Location of company headquarters: ______________________

Website for company: ____

Reasons to invest in the company: ____

Reasons not to invest: ____

Name ________________________________ Date __________ Class ____________________

Lesson 21.5 Develop a Business Plan

LESSON QUIZ

Directions For each of the following statements, if the statement is true, write a T on the answer line; if the statement is false, write an F on the answer line.

_____ 1. Entrepreneurs should have help readily available when problems are encountered and decisions must be made.

_____ 2. The business plan contains the information used and the initial decisions made to manage each of the major areas of a business.

_____ 3. A business plan is helpful only to the entrepreneur and not other people involved in starting the business.

_____ 4. A business plan should not be shared with the employees of a business.

_____ 5. A business plan is more effective if it contains a general outline of business operations rather than specific decisions for each part of the business.

_____ 6. A business plan should include financial projections for income, expenses, profit, and the return on investment that investors can expect.

_____ 7. The first step in preparing a business plan is to develop a one- or two-page executive summary.

Directions For each of the following items, decide which choice best completes the statement. Write the letter that identifies your choice on the answer line.

_____ 8. Every business plan should contain
A. a description of the sources of financing
B. a description of the type of competition the business will face
C. a description of employees the business will need
D. all of the above

_____ 9. A business plan should be provided to
A. investors and the company's bankers
B. customers
C. major competitors
D. all of the above

_____10. The executive summary of a business plan provides
A. a detailed description of all business activities
B. complete financial projections
C. a resume of the business owner
D. highlights of the major planning decisions

_____11. The Market Analysis section of the business plan contains a description of
A. economic conditions
B. the marketing mix
C. target markets
D. long and short-term objectives

Activity 1 • Summarize a Business Plan

Directions Choose a business you would like to start. Assume you have already prepared a detailed business plan for your new company. Answer each of the following questions to provide information that would be included in a two-page executive summary.

Name of business: ______________________________ Location: __________________________

Description of products and services: ____

____

Name(s) of owner(s): ____

Form of ownership: ____

Key business objectives: ____

____

Major strengths: ____

____

Main weakness: ____

____

Current economic environment: ____

Main competitors: ____

Description of target market: ____

Main/unique needs of the target market: ____

Major activities of the organization: ____

Important resources needed: ____

____

Staffing requirements: ____

____

Description of marketing mix: ____

____

Important startup costs: ____

____

Other financial resources needed: ____

____

Sources of financing: ____

____

Name ____ Date ___________ Class______________________

Lesson 22.1 The Functions of Management

LESSON QUIZ

Directions For each of the following statements, if the statement is true, write a T on the answer line; if the statement is false, write an F on the answer line.

_____ 1. Effective managers are able to organize the resources and work of a company in ways that result in success.

_____ 2. Staffing is considered the most easily accomplished of the management functions.

_____ 3. Implementing a marketing strategy effectively requires both people and other resources.

_____ 4. The work of managers is classified into three functions: planning, implementing, and evaluating.

_____ 5. Long-range planning involves setting broad goals and direction.

_____ 6. Short-term planning is also known as operational planning.

_____ 7. Controlling is the ability to communicate the direction of the business and to influence others to successfully carry out the needed work.

Directions For each of the following items, decide which choice best completes the statement. Write the letter that identifies your choice on the answer line.

_____ 8. Marketing managers are successful when
A. the marketing plan is completed
B. all marketing jobs are filled
C. all products are sold
D. customers are satisfied and the company is profitable

_____ 9. Marketing managers are responsible for
A. identifying target markets and planning marketing mixes
B. manufacturing the product
C. providing the revenues needed by the business
D. all of the above

_____10. The activities needed to match individuals with the work to be done are known as
A. organizing
B. staffing
C. leading
D. controlling

_____11. Managers use these activities when they measure performance, compare it with goals and objectives, and make adjustments when necessary.
A. organizing
B. staffing
C. leading
D. controlling

Activity 1 • Manage Your Time

Directions Interview a manager of a local business and determine in an average week how much of the manager's time is spent on each of the five management functions. Prepare a pie chart in the space below that illustrates the percentage of an average work week spent on each function. Bring your findings to class and share them with your classmates. How are they the same or different? Combine your results with other class members to determine averages for all managers. What conclusions can you draw from your findings and those of your classmates?

Activity 2 • Manage in Fives

Directions For each of the following management functions, list five activities that a marketing manager might perform.

Planning: ____________________

____

____

Organizing: ____________________

____

____

Staffing: ____________________

____

____

Leading: ____________________

____

____

Controlling: ____________________

____

____

Name ______________________________ Date __________ Class ____________________

Lesson 22.2 Manage with a Marketing Plan

LESSON QUIZ

Directions For each of the following statements, if the statement is true, write a T on the answer line; if the statement is false, write an F on the answer line.

_____ 1. Successful companies develop and follow written business plans.

_____ 2. A marketing plan serves as a long-range plan that sets goals and direction for the company for the length of time that the plan is in effect.

_____ 3. The market analysis portion of a marketing plan provides detailed information for managers about the specific activities they need to perform.

_____ 4. The marketing strategy section of a marketing plan describes the competition and the economy.

_____ 5. Much of the organizing work in a company should be done after a marketing plan is developed.

_____ 6. Marketing effectiveness means that both the customers and the business are satisfied.

_____ 7. All business organizations are created for the purpose of making a profit.

Directions For each of the following items, decide which choice best completes the statement. Write the letter that identifies your choice on the answer line.

_____ 8. A company will not want to change its basic organizational structure unless
- A. it sees ways to improve performance or save money with the change.
- B. a manager leaves the company
- C. all managers agree to the organizational change
- D. all of the above

_____ 9. A(n) ____________________ specifies the minimum level of expected performance for an activity.
- A. business plan
- B. performance standard
- C. organizational objective
- D. effectiveness measure

_____10. A group of employees who work together toward a common purpose or goal without the usual managerial supervision is a(n)
- A. department
- B. marketing team
- C. self-directed work team
- D. entrepreneurial organization

Activity 1 • Advertise Your Philosophy

Directions Often companies use an important organizational or management policy or philosophy in headlines or taglines for their promotional campaigns. An example of this is General Electric's focus on innovation using "Innovation = Imagination" as a promotional theme. Look through current magazines and newspapers and identify three advertisements that use a management philosophy in their promotional copy. Cut out these advertisements and paste them on a sheet of paper. Answer the following questions about each ad.

1. What is the organizational or management philosophy or policy being emphasized?
2. How does the company expect to benefit by using this philosophy or policy in its advertising?

Activity 2 • From Problems to Plans

Directions Planning and controlling are interrelated management functions. In reviewing performance results, managers identify problems and issues that lead to planning activities. For the following general business problems, write a specific planning activity for the company designed to address the problem.

1. Sales volume has been declining at all stores on the east side of the city. ____________________

   ____

   ____

2. Operating supply costs have increased 10 percent in one year.____________________

   ____

   ____

3. Employee accidents are increasing among persons employed more than five years.__________

   ____

   ____

4. Customer surveys indicate customers would like the store to stay open later in the evenings._

   ____

   ____

   ____

5. Supervisors report that employee morale seems to be low.____________________

   ____

   ____

   ____

6. Employees are leaving the company for higher salaries at other businesses.________________

   ____

   ____

   ____

Name ______________________________ Date __________ Class ____________________

Lesson 22.3 The Marketing Manager Role

LESSON QUIZ

Directions For each of the following statements, if the statement is true, write a T on the answer line; if the statement is false, write an F on the answer line.

_____ 1. Managers are involved in identifying the need for personnel and filling those positions with the most qualified people.

_____ 2. A marketing executive spends most planning time on quarterly, monthly, and weekly plans.

_____ 3. Procedures are the steps to be followed for consistent performance of important activities.

_____ 4. Most sales managers are very active in training salespeople and helping them improve their selling skills.

_____ 5. Top managers have more leadership responsibilities than lower-level managers.

_____ 6. All managers must be able to involve people in planning, communicate expectations, and build effective teams to accomplish work.

_____ 7. Managers need to be able to recognize performance that contributes to the goals of the company and provide rewards to encourage people to perform well.

Directions For each of the following items, decide which choice best completes the statement. Write the letter that identifies your choice on the answer line.

_____ 8. Marketing activities in a company can be organized by
A. geographic locations
B. type of market
C. product category
D. all of the above

_____ 9. Rules or guidelines to be used in a company to make consistent decisions are
A. plans
B. procedures
C. policies
D. standards

_____10. The major controlling activity of managers is to
A. gather and review information to determine if objectives, plans, and standards are met
B. develop the standards for performance of the company's marketing activities
C. correct mistakes that cause marketing problems
D. revise the marketing plan

Activity 1 • Staffing and Compensation Planning

Directions Use the information provided to develop a work schedule for a store and to answer the questions that follow.

Sarah Mendez is opening a gift boutique. The store will be open Monday through Friday: 10:00 a.m. until 8:00 p.m.; Saturday: 10:00 a.m. until 5:00 p.m; and closed on Sunday. Sarah plans to work every day until 5:00, and she needs one full-time person for each of the days, 10:00 until 5:00. She also needs two part-time employees at night from 4:00 until 9:00. On Saturday, she wants two employees to work from opening until one hour past closing. She has decided to hire the following people.

José—can work after 3:00 p.m. on Mondays, Wednesdays, and Fridays

Tara—can work 10:00 until 5:00 every day except Thursdays

Jim—can work every Saturday and Tuesday night

Linda—can work every other Saturday and all day Mondays and Thursdays

Fred—can work every evening after 4:00

Ann—can work every other Saturday and one or two days during the week until 5:00

1. Complete the following work schedule for the boutique by identifying the days and times each employee will work.

	Mon.	Tues.	Wed.	Thurs.	Fri.	Sat.
10:00						
11:00						
12:00						
1:00						
2:00						
3:00						
4:00						
5:00						
6:00						
7:00						
8:00						
9:00						

2. Are all work days currently covered with the necessary number of employees? ____________

3. If not, what else does Sarah need? ____

____

4. If Sarah pays a wage rate of $7.55 per hour to each employee and pays herself $350 per week, what will be her total weekly wage and salary costs based on the number of hours currently covered?

____

Name ______________________ Date __________ Class ______________

Lesson 23.1 Benefits of a Marketing Career

LESSON QUIZ

Directions For each of the following statements, if the statement is true, write a T on the answer line; if the statement is false, write an F on the answer line.

_____ 1. Marketing is less important to businesses today than it was in the past.

_____ 2. Marketing jobs are found at the lowest and highest levels of a company and are available for people with varied amounts of education and experience.

_____ 3. Marketing jobs are found in only one-fourth to one-third of all businesses.

_____ 4. A career is a chosen area of work, usually made up of a progression of jobs, that provides personal and professional satisfaction.

_____ 5. Many large U.S. companies have CEOs who started their business careers in marketing.

_____ 6. As companies develop new products and services for identifying new market opportunities, marketers are involved from the beginning.

_____ 7. When economic conditions are poor, marketing employees are often the first to be reduced and the last to be rehired.

Directions For each of the following items, decide which choice best completes the statement. Write the letter that identifies your choice on the answer line.

_____ 8. In the United States, marketing jobs are
A. about 15 percent of all jobs
B. between 25–33 percent of all jobs
C. nearly 50 percent of all jobs
D. more than 75 percent of all jobs

_____ 9. __________________ is an ongoing process involving self assessment, career exploration, and decision making leading to a satisfying career decision.
A. Career education
B. Personal development
C. Career planning
D. Job preparation

_____10. The most common reason why a person is not considered when a position is filled in an organization is
A. lack of appropriate preparation
B. unreasonable compensation requests by the potential employee
C. geographic limitations
D. disability

Activity 1 • Analyze Career Requirements

Directions Picture the career position you would like to have 10 years from now. It does not have to be a marketing position. Use the library or Internet to find more information about the position and the preparations you need to complete to hold the position. Answer the following questions.

Job title: ______________________________ Salary range: ____________________

Main duties and responsibilities: ____

____

____

Is it a marketing career? Yes _____ No _____

How can marketing skills benefit you in the career? ______________________________

____

Important skills needed: ____

____

____

Education required: ____

____

Experience required: ____

____

Two companies you would like to work for that have this position: ____________________

____

Activity 2 • Marketing Is Everywhere

Directions Using newspapers and the Internet, locate companies and job opportunities that fit each of the following criteria:

A marketing company with a marketing job:

Company ______________________ Job title: ______________________

A non-marketing company with a marketing job:

Company ______________________ Job title: ______________________

A nonprofit organization with a marketing job:

Company ______________________ Job title: ______________________

An international company with a marketing job:

Company ______________________ Job title: ______________________

A marketing company with a non-marketing job:

Company ______________________ Job title: ______________________

Name ______________________________ Date __________ Class ______________

Lesson 23.2 Employment Levels in Marketing

LESSON QUIZ

Directions For each of the following statements, if the statement is true, write a T on the answer line; if the statement is false, write an F on the answer line.

_____ 1. Career planning increases your chances for a successful career.

_____ 2. The knowledge and skills needed to be successful in a job will not change over time.

_____ 3. A career path is a series of unrelated jobs all having similar knowledge and skill requirements.

_____ 4. A person's career plan will probably change several times.

_____ 5. People often do not view their entry-level position as the first step in a career path.

_____ 6. People in career-level positions usually view the work as more than a job to earn money.

_____ 7. Today, most career positions in marketing require only a high school degree.

Directions For each of the following items, decide which choice best completes the statement. Write the letter that identifies your choice on the answer line.

_____ 8. The levels of employment in marketing, in the correct sequence, are
A. entry, specialist, career, supervisor/manager, and executive/owner
B. entry, supervisor/manager, career, specialist, and executive/owner
C. specialist, career, entry, executive/owner, and supervisor/manager
D. entry, career, specialist, supervisor/manager, and executive/owner

_____ 9. Which of the following is not a foundational skill needed by marketers?
A. marketing functions
B. business principles
C. interpersonal and basic work skills
D. academic preparation

_____10. Interpersonal skills are important to marketers because they
A. work with people on their marketing team
B. communicate with customers to solve problems
C. are involved regularly with people inside and outside of the company
D. all of the above

_____11. Which specialized marketing skill also requires math, statistics, and computer skills?
A. product and service management
B. marketing information management
C. market planning
D. all of the above

Activity 1 • Marketing Communication

Directions Marketing communication is used in business for many purposes in addition to promoting and selling products. It is an important tool in resolving customer problems. You are a marketing supervisor presented with each of the following customer problems. Describe how you would use effective communications to resolve the customer's concern.

Roberta Flagg purchased a front-loading washer from your store. It is a model with many features she has not used before. After three attempts to use it, she is dissatisfied with the performance of the washer.

Jeffrey Smith has been in your store for 15 minutes. The store is very busy, and he feels your salespeople have ignored him and treated him rudely.

Grace Wilson recently purchased a dining room table from your furniture company's website that was delivered by another company. After it was delivered and set up in her dining room, she discovered a deep scratch on one of the table legs. The delivery personnel had already left when she found the problem.

Aston Jetta purchased a new computer from your store on Wednesday. Over the weekend, your store promoted a very similar model at a 15 percent price reduction. Aston wants to return his computer for the one being promoted. Your store has a policy that customers returning technology products that do not have defects are charged a 10 percent restocking fee. Aston doesn't think he should have to pay that fee because he should have been informed about the promotion.

Name ______________________________ Date __________ Class__________________

Lesson 23.3 Marketing Education and Career Paths

LESSON QUIZ

Directions For each of the following statements, if the statement is true, write a T on the answer line; if the statement is false, write an F on the answer line.

_____ 1. Many high schools offer business and marketing classes as electives designed to develop general knowledge of marketing principles.

_____ 2. A Marketing Education program incorporates three types of complementary learning experiences—introductory and advanced courses in marketing, business work experiences, and a student organization.

_____ 3. Community colleges offer Associate of Arts, Associate of Applied Science, and shorter certificate programs in marketing.

_____ 4. A Marketing Education program provides work experience.

_____ 5. If you earn a college degree, there will be no need for further study during your marketing career.

_____ 6. In recent years, businesses have reduced the number of levels of management and given the employees more responsibility and authority.

_____ 7. Management jobs provide the only means to get to the top in a marketing career.

Directions For each of the following items, decide which choice best completes the statement. Write the letter that identifies your choice on the answer line.

_____ 8. The international association of high school and college students studying marketing, management, and entrepreneurship in business, finance, hospitality, and marketing sales and service is

A. the Marketing Education Association
B. DECA
C. Junior Achievement
D. Business Students of America

_____ 9. Marketers can continue to educate themselves after employment by

A. earning a Master of Business Administration
B. attending conferences and seminars
C. reading business and marketing magazines
D. all of the above

_____10. If you select a career path in distribution, marketing-information management, risk management, or financing, your career path is based on

A. marketing functions
B. marketing industries
C. marketing career levels
D. marketing skills

Activity 1 • Organize Career Paths

Directions Match the job titles on the left with the correct career paths on the right. Organize the job titles in the correct sequence to illustrate a possible career path.

Project Leader Licensed Practical Nurse District Manager Battalion Chief Nurse Practitioner Department Manager Project Consultant Regional Director of Retail Operations Captain IT Manager Fire Chief Senior Programmer Registered Nurse Store Manager Vice President of Technology	**Nursing** Nurse's Aide ↓ ↓ ↓	**Firefighting** Firefighter ↓ ↓ ↓
	Retailing Customer Service Rep ↓ ↓ ↓ ↓	**Technology** Programming Intern ↓ ↓ ↓ ↓ ↓

Activity 2 • Career Possibilities

Directions For each marketing function listed below, list five possible jobs that relate to that function. Try to think of jobs in a variety of industries and at different career levels.

Function	Jobs
Promotion	
Distribution	
Pricing	
Selling	
Product Planning	

Name ______________________________ Date __________ Class ____________________

Lesson 23.4 Begin Career Planning

LESSON QUIZ

Directions For each of the following statements, if the statement is true, write a T on the answer line; if the statement is false, write an F on the answer line.

_____ 1. People often move into totally different areas of work than they originally planned.

_____ 2. Employers value experience because it demonstrates interest in business, motivation, interpersonal skills, and the ability to apply what they have learned in school.

_____ 3. It is not easy to find an entry-level job in marketing because the number of jobs is limited.

_____ 4. It is important that your career plan be very specific, even at the beginning.

_____ 5. Everything you do whether good or bad should be included in your career portfolio.

_____ 6. An electronic portfolio is similar to a traditional career portfolio except it is prepared, maintained, and saved using computer technology.

_____ 7. If you are offered a job after an interview but it does not fit your career plan, it is appropriate to decline the offer.

Directions For each of the following items, decide which choice best completes the statement. Write the letter that identifies your choice on the answer line.

_____ 8. You can add to work experience by
A. completing an internship
B. volunteering in community organizations
C. participating in school activities
D. all of the above

_____ 9. Which of the following is not a step in developing a career plan?
A. complete an assessment of your current knowledge, skills, and interests
B. identify the education and experience requirements for the marketing careers that interest you
C. complete a written job application
D. make a list of the knowledge and skills you will need to develop

_____10. A career portfolio
A. demonstrates your education and experience
B. contains information about jobs for which you have applied
C. identifies potential employers
D. all of the above

_____11. In order to complete a successful interview, you will need to
A. dress and look professional
B. bring a portfolio or select items from your portfolio
C. thank the interviewer
D. all of the above

Activity 1 • Job Application Worksheet

Directions Complete the following worksheet with information that can be used to help you with job applications. *(Some personal information required for most applications is not included to protect your privacy.)* After completing the worksheet, obtain a job application from a local business. Use the worksheet to complete the application and prepare a one-page letter to the company highlighting your qualifications for the job and requesting an interview.

Name: ______________________________ Address: ______________________________

Telephone: ____

My Career Objective: ____

Job Titles related to my Career Objective: ___________________________________

____

Academic Courses and Educational Experiences: _______________________________

____

Basic Employment Skills: ____

____

Specific Marketing Skills: ____

____

____

Paid and Non-Paid Work Experiences: ____

____

____

Volunteer Work and Community Service: ______________________________________

____

____

School Activities and Major Projects: ____

____

____

Leadership Roles and Teamwork: ____

____

____

Achievements and Recognition: ____

____

____